"Suffice it to say that the Lancaster, measured in no matter what terms, was, and still is, incomparably the most efficient. In range, bomb-carrying capacity, ease of handling, freedom from accident, and particularly in casualty rate, it far surpassed the other heavy types. Hence the constant pressure brought by HQ Bomber Command for concentration on Lancaster production at the expense of other types, and hence the policy to employ every available Lancaster in the front line, even at the expense of an uneconomical training set-up." (Sir Arthur Harris)

Lancaster PA474 of the Battle of Britain Memorial Flight (FP - Duncan Cubitt)

A special edition of *FlyPast* magazine, published October 1998

Editorial
Editor : **Ken Delve**
Assistant Editor : **Robert Rudhall**
Editor's Secretary : **Pauline Hughes**

Photography
Chief Photographer: **Duncan Cubitt**
Photographer: **Steve Fletcher**

Design
Design: **Mike Carr, David Robinson, Lee Howson, Austin Smith, Patrick Juggins**

Production
Production Editor: **Sue Blunt**
Production Manager : **David Sopher**

Advertising
Aviation Group Director : **John Barker**
Advertisement Manager : **Simon Patrick**
Administration: **Joanne Holt**

Marketing & Circulation
Manager : **John Phillips**

Publisher & Chief Executive
Richard Cox

Published by Key Publishing Ltd,
PO Box 100, Stamford, Lincs, PE9 1XQ, UK.
Tel: +44(0)1780 75513 Fax +44(0)1780 757261

http://www.keymags.co.uk

Distributed by
USM Distribution Limited, 86 Newman Street,
London W1P 3LD Tel: 0171 396 8000
Fax: 0171 396 8002 email: usm.co.uk

Printed by
Williams Gibbons Ltd Tel: 01902 730011

Typeset and composed by
Colortone, Stamford, Lincs. Tel: 01780 757676.

Colour Process by
County Graphics, Holwell, Hertfordshire.

Printed in England

Contents

6 .. **WIN the Ultimate Lancaster Experience**
Enter this competition, run in conjunction with FlyPast, for a chance to win a close-up look at the interiors of four surviving Lancasters — three in the UK and one in Canada.

8 .. **Lancaster at War**
Development and operational career of the Lancaster, includes.

26 .. **Re-sparring PA474**
The mammoth task of replacing the wing spars in the BBMF Lancaster.

34 .. **Displaying the Lanc**
Thoughts from the crews who display the two surviving airworthy aircraft.

40 .. **Hitler's Gremlins**
A series of aircraft crashes delays one Lancaster crewman reaching operational status.

44 .. **Survivors**
World round-up of surviving airframes.

52 .. Green Endorsement

It was not only the enemy who caused problems — a story of exceptional airmanship after a mid-air collision.

56 .. Lancaster Data

Production details, internal views colour artwork, 3-views.

60 .. Master Bomber

Dennis Witt started his career flying Whitleys and ended up as a Lancaster Master Bomber with the Pathfinder Force.

65 .. Recce Test

Identify the bombers and win a bundle of books.

66 .. For Valour

Of the 19 Victoria Crosses awarded to Bomber Command, ten went to Lancaster crewmen.

72 .. Lancasters over Canada

Postwar use of the Lancaster by the Royal Canadian Air Force.

79 .. French Connection

French Navy Lancaster operations.

The Ultimate Lancaster Experience

Here is a 'once in a lifetime' chance to inspect the interiors of four Avro Lancaster bombers, including both of the world's airworthy examples!

FlyPast has put together a package that will make every Lancaster fanatic's heart beat a little faster. The winner of this 'easy to enter' competition will be able to clamber around the innards of four Lancasters — three in the UK and one in Canada.

The prize starts with a look around the Imperial War Museum's Lancaster B.X KB889, preserved in static condition at Duxford, Cambs. Then there's the opportunity to be on board Lancaster B.VII NX611 (G-ASXX) as it gives one of its

A view from the cockpit of Lancaster 'KB726' as she rumbles across the Canadian countryside. (FP - Robert Rudhall)

The Canadian Warplane Heritage's 'Lanc' 'KB726' is celebrating its tenth year of flying operations with the museum this year. (FP - Duncan Cubitt)

popular taxi demonstrations organised by the Lincolnshire Aviation Heritage Centre at East Kirkby, Lincs.

Not very far away, at RAF Coningsby, is Europe's only airworthy 'Lanc', the Battle of Britain Memorial Flight's B.I PA474. The

winner will enjoy a guided tour of this famous bomber's interior. Very few people get the chance see the inside this stalwart of the British airshow circuit!

The icing on the cake is a trip to Canada to climb aboard the world's other airworthy

Lancaster, B.X 'KB726' (C-GVRA) operated by Canadian Warplane Heritage (CWH). Flown on a regular basis, this 'Lanc' is indeed a rarity, it being the only flyable example of the breed in private ownership. During the trip to the CWH the winner

The most well known of the airworthy Lancasters is the Battle of Britain Memorial Flight's PA474. (FP - Duncan Cubitt)

The nerve centre of Lancaster PA474. (FP - Duncan Cubitt)

Experience, PO Box 100, Stamford, Lincs, PE9 1XQ, England. Closing date for entries is January 1, 1999. The first completed coupon with all three tokens, and the correct answer, drawn out of the 'hat' on that date will be declared the winner. And the very best of luck!

This competition is organised by Key Exhibitions Ltd. The prize on offer is as stated. There is no cash equivalent and no correspondence will be entered into.

If you have not managed to obtain copies of the October and November issues of FlyPast then contact our Mail Order Department at the FlyPast address.

The interior of KB889 is in 100% original condition. (FP - Robert Rudhall)

The Imperial War Museum's KB889 is a fine static example of Britain's famous wartime bomber. (FP - Duncan Cubitt)

will also have the opportunity to view the other historic aircraft in this world-renowned collection (see last month's *FlyPast* for a rundown of what is in store at the CWH Museum).

It is unlikely that a prize of this nature could ever be arranged again, so do not miss this opportunity!

All you have to do is answer the easy question (printed on the coupon attached to the October issue of *FlyPast*) and collect three tokens — the last of which is printed here (the first appeared in the October issue and the second in the November *FlyPast*). When you have all three tokens, stick them onto the coupon and send it to: Lancaster

Lancaster B.VII NX611 'Just Jane' at East Kirkby is maintained in ground running condition. (FP - Robert Rudhall)

Token no. 3

Token 3
TER

Lancaster - The Operational Record

Lancasters of 57 Squadron over the target — painting by Michael Turner.

WHEN WAR BROKE out in September 1939 the RAF's offensive element, Bomber Command, was equipped with a variety of twin-engined aircraft, most of which carried an average 4,000lb (1,800kg) bomb load and were designed to visually attack their targets in daylight. Within a matter of months, the vulnerability of these bombers to enemy fighters meant that Bomber Command had to transfer the bulk of its operations to the cover of night. Over the next two years the Command waged its war, with limited success, against German industrial cities. Early 1942 brought two significant developments — the entry into service of the Avro Lancaster and the appointment of Arthur Harris as Commander-in-Chief of Bomber Command. Significant expansion plans and the adoption of four-engined types such as the Lancaster, Halifax and Stirling, were already in place when Harris took over in February; Bomber Command had a bomb lift of 510 tons. By January 1945 the position had dramatically altered, the bomb lift had risen to 5,264 tons; of the 105 squadrons, 62 1/2 of which were equipped with Lancasters. Whilst the Vickers Wellington had shouldered the bulk of the campaign for the first three years, and other types such as the Halifax had key roles to

The Avro Lancaster is widely accepted as being the most effective Allied bomber of World War Two; in the latter stages of the war it dominated the strength of Bomber Command's Main Force. Ken Delve outlines its career.

play, it was the Lancaster that came to symbolise the striking power of Bomber Command.

In his post-war 'Despatch on War Operations', Sir Arthur Harris paid tribute to the Lancaster: "The Lancaster, however, coming into operation for the first time on March 10/11, 1942, soon proved immensely superior to all other types in the Command. The advantage which it enjoyed in speed, height and range enabled it to attack with success targets which other types could attempt only with serious risk or even certainty of heavy casualties. Their high performance was a tremendous asset, but as yet their numbers were totally inadequate to deliver the concentrated attacks necessary to saturate defended objectives."

As 1942 opened, the majority of the Command's effort was still being expended on the anti-naval campaign with attacks on U-boat construction sites — the Battle of the Atlantic was at a crucial phase and it was essential to the war effort that the convoys losses be reduced. Part of the

anti-naval campaign involved mine-laying and Bomber Command aircraft had begun to play an increasing part in this task. On March 3/4 Bomber Command sent 235 aircraft to attack the Renault factory at Billancourt near Paris, employing a new flare marking tactic in an effort to improve bombing accuracy. The attack was considered to be a major success — however, the night was also significant from the point of view of our story as the first operational outing for the Avro Lancaster. Four aircraft from 44 Squadron were tasked to lay mines off the German coast. Each aircraft dropped four mines from 600ft (180m) — L7546 (Sqn Ldr Nettleton) and L7568 (Flt Lt Sandford) at 'Yams' (the Heligoland Approaches) and L7549 (W/O Crum) and L7547 (W/O Lamb) at 'Rosemary' (Heligoland). The mission was uneventful.

A week later the Squadron sent three aircraft on the Lancaster's first bombing mission, as part of a force of 126 aircraft attacking Essen. The first of the Lancs over the target was L7536 (Fg Off Ball) at

and gave chase. In a 30-minute combat, all three Lancasters in Nettleton's second section were shot down.

The fighters then turned on the lead section and the No 3 aircraft was soon downed; both the other aircraft were also hit but the fighters then had to break off and return to base. Nettleton and his sole remaining colleague pressed on to the target; the second Lancaster was hit by flak and crashed just after releasing its bombs. Nettleton was the sole survivor from the 44 Sqn flight and made his lonely way home. The six aircraft from 97 Sqn had reached the target unscathed and made their attacks, each section losing one aircraft to the intense light flak. Seven of the 12 aircraft had been shot down and of the 85 men who had taken part in the raid, 49 were missing (it was later revealed that 12 had survived to become PoWs). A

striking power. The night of May 30/31 saw 1,047 bombers attack Cologne — the gathering of this huge armada was a major achievement with operational squadrons and OTUs (Operational Training Units) pulling out all the stops to put up the maximum number of aircraft. No 5 Gp contributed 73 Lancasters to the total effort, one of which failed to return.

The Cologne attack was the first operational outing for 61 Squadron's Lancasters — and they had only begun converting to type three weeks previously. It was the seventh Lancaster squadron, nos 83, 50, 106 and now 61 having joined the original three squadrons of No 5 Gp.

The success of this raid was also the first serious loss of prestige to Goering, from which he, and the Luftwaffe, never fully recovered in the eyes of Hitler. Within a year it was

The groundcrew, as here with a 550 Squadron Lancaster, performed near miracles to achieve high serviceability rates, especially when 'maximum efforts' were tasked — painting by Michael Turner. (Details of Michael's art prints can be obtained from: Studio 88 Ltd, PO Box 88, Chesham, Bucks HP5 2SR.)

number of bombs hit the target and production was reduced for a few weeks — although the exact extent of the damage has never been revealed. John Nettleton was awarded the Victoria Cross for his leadership and despite the losses, the raid was considered a success. Harris later had this to say: "The carefully-planned attack on the MAN works at Augsburg in which seven out of 12 Lancasters were lost, showed the impracticability of daylight operations against Germany in anything but small numbers and on rare occasion, without long-range fighter cover."

The Command continued to attack industrial cities in May, with mixed fortunes. Bomber Command still had it detractors and Harris was determined to show what could be achieved if his Command was given adequate

the Lancaster that became, to the German leaders and people, and the British public, THE Allied bomber that came night after night. As with the Spitfire/Hurricane comparison in the Battle of Britain this was, of course, an inaccurate over-simplification — but it was very much the position at the time.

Two more 'thousand bomber' attacks were made — 956 aircraft (74 Lancasters) hitting Essen on June 1/2 and 1,067 aircraft (96 Lancasters) attacking Bremen on June 25/26. It was impossible to keep the bomber concentration together any longer as it was having a detrimental effect on training, with the OTUs having to put a major effort into this operational scenario. The training system was in need of re-organisation and

No 101 Sqn
"Mens agitat molem" (Mind over matter)
Marks:	I, III
Dates:	Oct 1942 - Aug 1946
Group:	1 Gp
Bases:	Holme on Spalding Moor, Ludford Magna, Binbrook
First Raid:	Nov 20/21, 1942 (Turin)
Operational Losses:	113
Unit Code:	SR

No 103 Sqn
"Noli me tangere" (Touch me not)
Marks:	I, III
Dates:	Oct 1942 - Nov 1945
Group:	1 Gp
Bases:	Elsham Wolds
First Raid:	Nov 21/22, 1942 (mine laying)
Operational Losses:	135
Unit Code:	PM

No 106 Sqn
"Pro libertate" (For freedom)
Marks:	I, III
Dates:	May 1942 - Feb 1946
Group:	5 Gp
Bases:	Coningsby, Syerston, Metheringham
First Raid:	May 30/31, 1942 (Cologne)
Operational Losses:	105
Unit Code:	ZN
Victoria Cross:	Sgt N C Jackson (air engineer)

No 109 Sqn
"Primi hastati" (The first of the legion)
Marks:	I
Dates:	May - Oct 1942
Group:	8 (PFF) Gp
Base:	Wyton
Note:	Partial temporary equipment for a primarily Mosquito equipped unit
Victoria Cross:	Sqn Ldr R A M Palmer DFC (pilot) [posthumous] flying a Lancaster of 582 Sqn

No 115 Sqn
"Despite the elements"
Marks:	I, II, III, I (FE)
Dates:	Mar 1943 - Jan 1950
Group:	3 Gp
Bases:	East Wretham, Little Snoring, Witchford, Graveley, Stradishall, Mildenhall
First Raid:	Mar 20/21, 1943 (mine laying)
Operational Losses:	110
Unit Codes:	KO, A2 ('C' Flt), IL ('C' Flt)

No 138 Sqn
"For Freedom"
Marks:	I, III
Dates:	Mar 1945 - Sep 1947
Group:	3 Gp
Bases:	Tuddenham, Wyton
First Raid:	Mar 29, 1945 (Salzgetter)
Operational Losses:	1
Unit Codes:	AC, NF

No 148 Sqn
"Trusty"
Marks:	I
Dates:	Nov 1946 - Jan 1950
Group:	3 Gp
Base:	Upwood
Unit Code:	AU

No 149 Sqn
"Fortis nocte" (Strong by night)
Marks:	I, III
Dates:	Aug 1944 - Nov 1949
Group:	3 Gp
Bases:	Methwold, Tuddenham, Stradishall, Mildenhall
First Raid:	Sep 17, 1944 (Boulogne)
Operational Losses:	4
Unit Codes:	OJ, TK ('C' Flt)

expansion as Bomber Command began to put in place its long-cherished plan for a front-line strength of 4,000 heavy bombers.

The combat record of the Command's aircraft was analysed by the Operational Research Section and by July they were expressing concern over both the Manchester and the Halifax; the latter being the subject of the following report that looked at the experience levels of pilots in No 4 Gp... "There is no reasonable doubt that pilots on their first two operations have a casualty rate well above the average and that those who had survived 20 sorties had a rate well below the average. This must be aircraft-related as the Lancaster does not suffer the same problem. New pilots are a bit nervous of the aircraft, the aircraft having gained a bad name for instability in manoeuvres. It thus may happen that a new pilot is reluctant when he meets defences to manoeuvre his machine sufficiently in combat or that in a

targets miles away — including Denmark.

The first success for the Pathfinders came on August 28/29 when 159 bombers, led by PFF aircraft, attacked Nuremberg. The Pathfinders dropped a new marker, called 'Red Blob Fire', and the results seemed reasonable — although 23 bombers failed to return (including four Lancasters). Bomber Command was slowly becoming more effective — but so were the German defences, especially the night fighters, and loss rates were to cause concern for the rest of the year, although the Lancaster invariably suffered the lowest percentage losses on Main Force raids. Lancaster losses, however, were not light and some squadrons seemed to be suffering quite badly — 9 Squadron, for example, flew its first Lancaster mission on September 10/11 (Düsseldorf); in its first four missions it lost six aircraft.

The Lancaster force continued to be tasked

— only to be pounced on by three Ar 196s, two of these were shot down. In all, 140 tons of bombs had been dropped on the target and damage was assessed as moderate.

Less than a week later, No 5 Group's Lancasters mounted a daylight raid on Milan, Italy. The force of 88 bombers flew individual routes across France to a rendezvous point at Lake Annecy before crossing the Alps. Once again the daring tactic had worked and only one aircraft was lost over the target, two others falling over France.

This was followed by a series of night raids on Italian cites — Turin, Genoa and Milan — in the autumn. Lancaster deliveries were accelerating and more squadrons had re-equipped by late October to bring the average availability of 'serviceable aircraft with crews' to almost the 200 mark.

At the November War Cabinet's Chiefs of Staff Committee there was wide-ranging

August 1941, Lancaster prototype with four Merlin XX engines. (FP Collection)

sudden emergency he puts the machine into an attitude in which he has had no previous experience of controlling it." By implication, Lancaster pilots did not feel such reluctance and were quite happy to throw their aircraft around.

The Pathfinder Force (PFF) was officially formed on August 11, 1942, under the command of Gp Capt Don Bennett. Discussions had been taking place since the spring regarding the creation of a specialist target-marking force, a move that Harris was initially against as he was wary of creating an elitist organisation that would drain the bomber Groups of their most experienced leaders and crews. The need, however, to improve bombing accuracy and the development of new navigation aids finally prompted the move and the PFF was established — the initial strength of five squadrons including two Lancaster units — 83 Squadron and 109 Squadron, the latter was essentially a Mosquito unit but had a number of Lancs for Oboe trials. The first PFF operation was flown on August 18/19 with 31 Pathfinder aircraft as part of a 118 bomber force attacking Flensburg. It was not a good start; met winds were inaccurate and a number of the PFF aircraft bombed

with special missions in addition to its contribution to Main Force. In July the Air Staff had tasked Bomber Command with attacking selected key armament works in France; the first attack on one of these targets was made on October 17 — day, low level by Lancasters of No 5 Gp, the target being the Schneider Armament and Locomotive works at Le Creusot. The Lancaster squadrons flew low-level practice sorties around the UK as part of the build-up for this hazardous mission. On the afternoon of October 17, 94 Lancasters took off, flew low-level over the Channel and sped on into France; one crew member recorded the scene... "At the height we were flying we disturbed the cattle in the fields and numbers of them stampeded. At one place we saw oxen bolt, dragging their plough after them. Many of the French peasants in the fields waved to us as we swept over."

The bombers met no opposition, much to their surprise, and only two aircraft from the Main Force received light damage from flak in the target area; of the six Lancasters briefed to attack a nearby power station, one was shot down by flak. The only other casualty was the Flight Engineer on a 97 Squadron Lancaster that had turned back early

discussion on the status of, and future potential for, the Strategic Bombing Offensive. It was considered that, "a heavy bomber force rising from 4,000 to 6,000 heavy bombers in 1944 could shatter the industrial and economic structure of Germany to a point where an Anglo-American force of reasonable strength could enter the Continent from the West." This force of 6,000 bombers would have a bomb lift of 90,000 tons per mission and 58 German towns were earmarked for destruction. Harris and Bomber Command had come a long way in 1942 for such a positive forward-looking statement to be made by the War Cabinet. The RAF's part of this heavy bomber force would comprise the Lancaster and Halifax, with the former taking the major role.

The Storm Breaks

By February 1943 Bomber Command was fielding 17 Lancaster squadrons, two of these being PFF (now called No 8 Gp) units, out of a total strength of 65 front-line squadrons, the majority of which were equipped with the Wellington or Halifax. By the end of the year the Lancaster total would increase to 30+ squadrons. A new

No 150 Sqn
"Always ahead" (Greek script)

Marks:	I, III
Dates:	Nov 1944 - Nov 1945
Group:	No 1
Bases:	Fiskerton, Hemswell
First Raid:	Nov 11/12, 1944 (Harburg)
Operational Losses:	6
Unit Code:	IQ

No 153 Sqn
"Noctivdus" (Seeing by night)

Marks:	I, III
Dates:	Oct 1944 - Sep 1945
Group:	1 Gp
Bases:	Kirmington, Scampton
First Raid:	Oct 7, 1944 (Emmerich)
Operational Losses:	22
Unit Code:	P4

No 156 Sqn
"We light the way"

Marks:	I, III
Dates:	Jan 1943 - Sep 1945
Group:	8 (PFF) Gp
Bases:	Upwood, Wyton
First Raid:	Jan 26/27, 1943 (Lorient)
Operational Losses:	104
Unit Code:	GT

No 166 Sqn
"Tenacity"

Marks:	I, III
Dates:	Sep 1943 - Nov 1945
Group:	1 Gp
Base:	Kirmington
First Raid:	Sep 22/23, 1943
Operational Losses:	114
Unit Code:	AS

No 170 Sqn
"Vidre non videri" (To see and not to be seen)

Marks:	I, III
Dates:	Oct 1944 - Nov 1945
Group:	1 Gp
Bases:	Kelstern, Dunholme Lodge, Hemswell
First Raid:	Oct 19/20, 1944
Operational Losses:	13
Unit Code:	TL

No 186 Sqn
(no badge/motto)

Marks:	I/III
Dates:	Oct 1944 - Jul 1945
Group:	3 Gp
Bases:	Tuddenham, Stradishall
First Raid:	Oct 18, 1944 (Bonn)
Operational Losses:	8
Unit Codes:	XY, AP ('C' Flt)

No 189 Sqn
(no badge/motto)

Marks:	I, III
Dates:	Oct 1944 - Nov 1945
Group:	5 Gp
Bases:	Bardney, Fulbeck, Metheringham
First Raid:	Nov 1, 1944 (Homburg)
Operational Losses:	16
Unit Code:	CA

No 195 Sqn
"Velocitate fortis" (Strong by speed)

Marks:	I, III
Dates:	Oct 1944 - Aug 1945
Group:	3 Gp
Bases:	Witchford, Wratting Common
First Raid:	Oct 26, 1944 (Leverkusen)
Operational Losses:	14
Unit Codes:	A4, JE ('C' Flt)

Lancaster variant entered service in January when 61 Squadron flew the first sorties with the Hercules-powered Lancaster II.

The bombers had closed 1942 with a series of attacks on German cities and Harris wished to continue this into 1943 — although on January 14 he was issued a new Directive giving U-boat bases in France as the top priority — but not at the expense of attacks on Berlin and other selected German cities.

Berlin was visited on the night of January 16/17 by a force of 201 bombers, primarily Lancasters from No 5 Gp; this was the first operational employment of purpose-designed Target Indicators (TIs). Berlin was attacked again the following night by 187 bombers, 22 being lost, including 19 Lancasters — a

weapons and the force capable of destroying the heart of the enemy's armament industry."

Thus commenced what has been called the Battle of the Ruhr, an attempt to cause critical damage to the German industrial heartland. In the period up to May, some 60% of the Command's effort was expended against targets in the Ruhr. The strike force included 18 Lancaster squadrons, some of which were in the process of re-equipping with the Lancaster III.

German night fighters continued to take a toll of the bomber streams but despite loss rates that from time to time equalled those of other types, the overall loss rate of Lancasters was less than had been anticipated and this, combined with deliveries of new aircraft, meant that there was a plentiful supply of aircraft

Based at Skellingthorpe, 50 Squadron re-equipped with Lancasters in May 1942. (Ken Delve Collection)

loss rate for the type of 11%, 9 and 12 Squadrons each lost four aircraft that night.

By early February the Command had a notional strength of 1,091 bombers, of which 642 were heavies — 119 Stirlings, 228 Halifaxes and 295 Lancasters. In addition to the other changes taking place, the first Bomber Command aircraft began to use another new blind-bombing device — H2S radar. The system was first employed on the Halifax but in due course the majority of the Command's bombers were equipped with the system.

In March 1943 Bomber Command launched a sustained offensive against targets in Germany — the first phase opened with an attack on Essen on March 5/6; 442 bombers being led by an Oboe-equipped Pathfinder force. The elusive industrial targets at Essen, so long virtually immune from severe damage, were hit hard and Harris commented: "Years of endeavour, of experiment, and of training in new methods have at last provided the

— and indeed crews as the HCUs were providing trained crews at a faster rate than squadrons could absorb them. There had been some concern as to the serviceability of the type, with a number of instances of low overall usage rates, and whilst this was being investigated the simple expedient of increasing the established strength of the squadrons eased the problem. By late spring, the Lancaster units were contributing over 200 bombers to major attacks, with some squadrons putting up as many as 18 aircraft.

By May the average 'contribution' had risen to over 300 aircraft, an indicator of the rapid nature of the re-equipment programme, an improvement in overall serviceability and the increase in UE (Unit Establishment) per squadron to 26+2 aircraft.

The Allied Commanders Conference held in Washington in May resulted in yet another new Directive (June 3) which brought into effect the Combined Bomber Offensive

With its distinctive modified bomb bay areas, this is one of the aircraft delivered to 617 Squadron for the Dams Raid, although it did not take part in the mission. (Ken Delve Collection)

(code-named 'Pointblank'), with the US 8th Air Force attacking strategic targets by day and Bomber Command covering the night period. Once again, much of this is beyond the scope of our survey.

The Dams Raid

The most famous incident of 1943, and the one that helped assure the Lancaster's place in history, was Operation 'Chastise' — the Dams Raid. The concept of causing industrial disruption by attacking certain critical dams had been in the British bombing plans for some time — back as far as the prewar Western Air plans. However, it was only with the advent of a suitable weapon that the plan became practicable. The weapon, and the impetus for the raid, came from one of Britain's most brilliant designers, Dr Barnes Wallis. After both theoretical and practical investigations, he concluded that the only way to cause critical damage to such structures was to explode a weapon against the inside face of the dam — underwater. The resultant shock wave would, in theory, cause structural failure of the dam. The

of operations to an incredible 174 missions).

By early May, Gibson had brought together and trained the crews that he required and the Lancasters had been modified to take the 'Upkeep' weapon (a mine rather then a bomb). It had not been easy, numerous problems had to be overcome with both the weapon and its delivery technique; but all of these had been solved by the May deadline date — the dams had to be attacked when the water level was still high. The attack plan was for 19 Lancasters, in three waves to attack the Mohne and Sorpe dams — Gibson leading nine aircraft would attack the former whilst five aircraft would attack the latter, the last wave of five aircraft was to act as an airborne reserve. The first wave took-off at 1650 hours on May 16 and few problems were encountered en route to the target, although one aircraft fell to flak and crashed near Dorsten. Gibson arrived over the Mohne just after midnight and made his run, scoring a good hit. Flt Lt Hopgood went in next but his aircraft was hit by flak and he dropped late, the mine bouncing over the dam and the Lancaster crashing soon afterwards — only two of the crew survived.

The first operational Lancaster unit was 44 Squadron at Waddington; this particular aircraft, R5556, went on to serve with 1661 HCU and crashed on May 13, 1943. (Ken Delve Collection)

special bomb would require a special, and accurate, delivery technique — and the creation of a specialist squadron. The man chosen to lead this unit, 617 Squadron, was Wg Cdr Guy Gibson, a very experienced bomber captain who had just finished his tour as CO of 106 Squadron (bringing his total

Gibson escorted the third aircraft, Flt Lt Martin, in order to divide the anti-aircraft fire. Martin's mine went short. Sqn Ldr Young was next and he was escorted in by both Gibson and Martin — to make an accurate delivery. The fifth attack was made by Flt Lt Maltby; the mine was again

No 207 Sqn
"Semper paratus" (Always prepared)

Marks:	I, III, I (FE)
Dates:	Mar 1942 - Aug 1949
Group:	5 Gp
Bases:	Bottesford, Langar, Spilsby, Methwold, Tuddenham, Stradishall, Mildenhall
First Raid:	Apr 24/25, 1942 (Rostock)
Operational Losses:	131
Unit Code:	EM

No 214 Sqn
"Ulter in Umbris" (Avenging in the shadows)

Mark:	B I (FE)
Dates:	Nov 1945 - Apr 1946 & Nov 1946 - Feb 1950
Group:	3 Gp
Bases:	Fayid (Egypt), Upwood
Unit Code:	QN

No 218 Sqn
"In time"

Marks:	I, III
Dates:	Aug 1944 - Aug 1945
Group:	3 Gp
Bases:	Methwold, Chedburgh
First Raid:	Sep 8, 1944 (Le Havre)
Operational Losses:	16
Unit Codes:	HA, XH ('C' Flt)

No 227 Sqn
no badge/motto

Marks:	I, III
Dates:	Oct 1944 - Sep 1945
Group:	5 Gp
Bases:	Bardney, Balderton, Strubby, Graveley
First Raid:	Oct 11, 1944 (Walcheren)
Operational Losses:	15
Unit Code:	9J

No 300 (Polish) Sqn
no motto

Marks:	I, III
Dates:	Apr 1944 - Oct 1945
Group:	1 Gp
Bases:	Faldingworth
First Raid:	Apr 18/19, 1944 (Rouen)
Operational Losses:	30
Unit Code:	BH

No 405 (Vancouver) Sqn RCAF
"Ducimus" (We lead)

Marks:	I, III, X
Dates:	Aug 1943 - Sep 1945
Group:	6 Gp, 8 (PFF) Gp
Bases:	Gransden Lodge, Linton-on-Ouse, Greenwood (Canada)
First Raid:	Aug 17/18, 1943 (Peenemünde)
Operational Losses:	50
Unit Code:	LQ

No 408 (Goose) Sqn RCAF
"For freedom"

Marks:	II, X
Dates:	Oct 1943 - Jul 1944 (Mk II) & May - Sep 1945 (Mk X)
Group:	6 Gp
Bases:	Linton-on-Ouse, Greenwood (Canada)
First Raid:	Oct 7/8, 1943 (Stuttgart) [Mk II]
Operational Losses:	41
Unit Code:	EQ

No 419 (Moose) Sqn RCAF
"Moose aswayita" (Beware of the moose)

Mark:	X
Dates:	Mar 1944 - Sep 1945
Group:	6 Gp
Bases:	Middleton St George, Yarmouth (Canada)
First Raid:	Apr 27/28, 1944 (Friedrichshafen)
Operational Losses:	39
Unit Code:	VR
Victoria Cross:	Plt Off A C Mynarki RCAF (air gunner) [posthumous]

No 420 (Snowy Owl) Sqn RCAF
"Pugnamus finitum" (We fight to a finish)

Mark:	X
Dates:	Apr - Sep 1945
Group:	6 Gp
Bases:	Tholthorpe, Debert (Canada)
Operational Losses:	nil - not used on operations
Unit Code:	PT

No 424 (Tiger) Sqn RCAF
"Castigandos castigamus"
(We chastise those who deserve to be chastised)

Marks:	I, III
Dates:	Jan - Oct 1945
Group:	6 Gp
Bases:	Skipton-on-Swale
First Raid:	Feb 1/2, 1945 (Ludwigshafen)
Operational Losses:	5
Unit Code:	QB

No 425 (Alouette) Sqn RCAF
"Je te plumerai" (I shall pluck you)

Mark:	X
Dates:	May - Sep 1945
Group:	6 Gp
Bases:	Tholthorpe, Debert (Canada)
Operational Losses:	nil - not used on operations
Unit Code:	KW

No 426 (Thunderbird) Sqn RCAF
"On wings of fire"

Mark:	II
Dates:	Jun 1943 - May 1944
Group:	6 Gp
Base:	Linton-on-Ouse
First Raid:	Aug 17/18, 1943 (Peenemünde)
Operational Losses:	28
Unit Code:	OW

No 427 (Lion) Sqn RCAF
"Ferte manus certas" (Strike sure)

Marks:	I, III
Dates:	Feb 1945 - May 1946
Group:	6 Gp
Base:	Leeming
First Raid:	Mar 11, 1945 (Essen)
Operational Losses:	nil
Unit Code:	ZL

No 428 (Ghost) Sqn RCAF
"Usque ad finem" (To the very end)

Mark:	X
Dates:	Jun 1944 - Sep 1945
Group:	6 Gp
Bases:	Middleton St George, Yarmouth (Canada)
First Raid:	July 7, 1944 (Normandy)
Operational Losses:	18
Unit Code:	NA

No 429 (Bison) Sqn RCAF
"Fortunae nihil" (Nothing to chance)

Marks:	I, III
Dates:	Mar 1945 - May 1946
Group:	6 Gp
Base:	Leeming
First Raid:	Apr 4/5, 1945 (Leuna)
Operational Losses:	1
Unit Code:	AL

well placed and as the attackers watched a crack appeared, followed by a large part of the centre of the dam crashing away and water pouring through. Gibson took those Lancasters still carrying mines on to the Eder Dam whilst the others were ordered to return to base.

The Eder Dam had no defences and so the Lancasters set up their attack pattern. Flt Lt Shannon's mine was accurate and caused a small breach. Sqn Ldr Maudslay placed his mine too long and his Lancaster was damaged by the explosion. The third attacker, Plt Off Knight put his mine in the right place and the Eder Dam collapsed outwards.

Meanwhile, the third wave had suffered badly — two aircraft had been forced to turn back early with technical problems and two others had been shot down en route, both probably victims of flak. The sole remaining Lancaster, that of Flt Lt McCarthy, pressed on to the Sorpe Dam and carried out an attack. The mine hit the dam — a different attack tactic was employed as this was an earth dam

619 Squadron formed at Woodhall Spa in April 1943. (Ken Delve Collection)

and not a standard concrete structure — but it caused little damage. The third wave also suffered two losses to flak, while a third aircraft had to abort the sortie. The remaining two pressed on, F/Sgt Brown attacked the Sorpe Dam and F/Sgt Townsend attacked the Ennepe Dam, both without result. Sadly, two more Lancasters were lost on the journey home — Sqn Ldr Young and Sqn Ldr Maudslay.

'Chastise' had undoubtedly been a great success; two of the primary targets had been breached, resulting in widespread damage from flooding (the results achieved by this attack have been the subject of 'hot' debate ever since they took place, some commentators claiming that they achieved nothing, whist others claim huge destruction and damage to morale). Damage to the German war industry certainly had been caused, albeit of short duration, and the British certainly scored a major propaganda coup. Losses had been high, with eight aircraft failing to return and 53 aircrew

being killed. Wg Cdr Guy Gibson was awarded a Victoria Cross for his "outstanding bravery and leadership during the raid", five officer pilots were awarded DSOs, the two NCO pilots received CGMs and other aircrew members received 15 DFCs and 12 DFMs. No 617 Squadron had not yet finished its specialist role — its Lancasters were to feature in a number of other spectacular missions before the war was over.

The Battle of the Ruhr was still in full swing with major attacks by formations of 800+ bombers on Dortmund, Düsseldorf, Cologne, Essen, Bochum, Wuppertal, Munster and Oberhausen. Amongst this series of attacks was that of June 19/20 against the Schneider and Breuil steelworks at Le Creusot — a night low-level visual bombing attack.

The following night saw No 5 Group's Lancasters fly the first of the so-called 'Shuttle' missions, with aircraft taking off from England to attack a target in southern Germany before flying on to land at airfields in Allied-held North Africa. The force of

60 Lancasters was tasked to attack the ex-Zeppelin works, now involved in the production of 'Wurzburg' early warning radars, at Friedrichshafen on the shores of Lake Constance. This was all part of Bomber Command's new Directive which called for attacks on the German aircraft industry, and fighter industry in particular, as both day and night fighters were causing heavy losses to Allied bombers.

One crew member recorded his view of the mission: "Approaching the French coast at 19,000ft, we encountered heavy cloud and electric storms up to 24,000ft. We therefore decided to come down below the front and lost height to 5,000ft. We were suddenly engaged by the defences of Caen or the outer defences of Le Havre — owing to technical difficulties with navigation instruments we were uncertain of our exact position. Four 4-gun heavy flak positions engaged us for about four minutes. During this time we altered course by about 30 degrees every 8 seconds, alternatively losing and gaining height by 1,000ft. The flak bursts were mainly 3-500ft behind and about the same distance above us. It was noticed that the rate of fire of the guns was extremely high! We flew on below cloud at 2,500-3,000ft across France and encountered no further opposition.

"Three-quarters of an hour's flying time from Lake Constance it was necessary to feather the port-inner engine, which was emitting showers of sparks, so we continued on three engines until we sighted the lake. By that time we had increased height to 6,000ft. As the port-inner engine is essential for the Mk XIV bombsight, it was unfeathered and allowed to windmill, but shortly afterwards the engine caught fire. We were

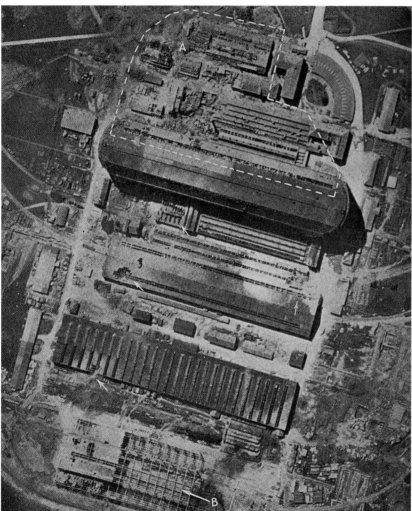

The former Zeppelin works at Friedrichshafen was the target for the first Lancaster 'shuttle raid', June 20/21, 1943. (Ken Delve Collection)

unable to feather it or extinguish the fire, which grew in intensity. The Captain then jettisoned the bombs, told the Deputy Leader to take over and gave the order to prepare to abandon the aircraft, first diving across the lake into Switzerland, and subsequently turning the aircraft towards Germany. We were about to bale out, expecting the petrol tanks to explode, when the engine seized and the fire went out. By this time we had descended to 4,000ft but were able to maintain height.

"We stayed over Lake Constance for 13 minutes and had an excellent view of the attack. There were approximately 16-20 heavy flak guns and 18-20 light flak guns, and 25 searchlights, within a radius of 6-8 miles of the target. Several aircraft were coned but not for any length of time. As the defences were heavier than expected, the Deputy Leader gave the order for all aircraft to increase height by 5,000ft, so that the attack was actually delivered from 10,000ft to 15,000ft. Leaving the target area, we commenced to fly over the Alps. By skirting the peaks we eventually crossed, gradually gaining height to 14,000ft. The 600-mile flight over the Mediterranean was slow, as we had to fly at 140mph to prevent over-heating. Eventually we sighted the Algerian coast and landed safely at Maison Blanche at 0752 — after a flight of 10 hours and 13 minutes."

The attack had been delivered by two waves of aircraft; the first following the PFF-laid TIs and the second using the technique of a 'timed run' from a visual point on the shore of the lake. The factories were hit and badly damaged. The attack had been 'directed' by Wg Cdr G L Gomm to keep the bombers on target — this use of a controlling aircraft, or Master Bomber,

No 431 (Iroquois) Sqn RCAF
"The hatiten ronteriios" (Warrior of the air)
Mark:	X
Dates:	Oct 1944 - Sep 1945
Group:	6 Gp
Bases:	Croft, Dartmouth (Canada)
First Raid:	Dec 17/18, 1944 (Duisberg)
Operational Losses:	11
Unit Code:	SE

No 432 (Leaside) Sqn RCAF
"Saeviter ad lucem" (Ferociously towards the light)
Mark:	II
Dates:	Oct 1943 - Feb 1944
Group:	6 Gp
Bases:	Skipton-on-Swale, East Moor
First Raid:	Nov 26/27, 1943 (Berlin)
Operational Losses:	8
Unit Code:	QO

No 433 (Porcupine) Sqn RCAF
"Qui s'y frotte s'y pique" (Who opposes it gets hurt)
Marks:	I, III
Dates:	Jan - Oct 1945
Group:	6 Gp
Base:	Skipton-on-Swale
First Raid:	Feb 1/2, 1945 (Ludwigshafen)
Operational Losses:	3
Unit Code:	BM

No 434 (Bluenose) Sqn RCAF
"In exelsis vincimus" (We conquer the heights)
Marks:	I, III, X
Dates:	Dec 1944 - Sep 1945
Group:	6 Gp
Bases:	Croft, Dartmouth (Canada)
First Raid:	Jan 2/3, 1945 (Nuremberg)
Operational Losses:	5
Unit Code:	WL

No 460 Sqn RAAF
"Strike and return"
Marks:	I, III
Dates:	Oct 1942 - Oct 1945
Group:	1 Gp
Bases:	Breighton, Binbrook, East Kirkby
First Raid:	Nov 22/23, 1942 (Stuttgart)
Operational Losses:	140
Unit Codes:	UV, AR

No 463 Sqn RAAF
"Press on regardless"
Marks:	I, III
Dates:	Nov 1943 - Sep 1945
Group:	5 Gp
Bases:	Waddington, Skellingthorpe
First Raid:	Nov 26/27, 1943 (Berlin)
Operational Losses:	69
Unit Code:	JO

No 467 Sqn RAAF
"Recidite adversarius atque ferocitea"
(To rain down with hostility and ferocity)
Marks:	I, III
Dates:	Nov 1942 - Sep 1945
Group:	5 Gp
Bases:	Scampton, Bottesford, Waddington, Metheringham
First Raid:	Jan 2/3, 1943 (mine laying)
Operational Losses:	104
Unit Code:	PO

No 514 Sqn
"Nil obstare potest" (Nothing can withstand)
Marks:	I, II, III
Dates:	Sep 1943 - Aug 1945
Group:	3 Gp
Bases:	Foulsham, Waterbeach
First Raid:	Sep 3/4, 1943 (Düsseldorf)
Operational Losses:	66
Unit Codes:	JI, A2 ('C' Flt)

would soon become standard for Bomber Command. No bombers were lost on this attack.

Three nights later, June 23/24, the Lancasters returned to the UK — bombing La Spezia on the way.

Hamburg was designated as a target to receive a concentrated series of attacks over a short period of time; under Operation 'Gomorrah'. The first of these, July 24/25, was also significant as it saw the first operational use of another defensive aid — 'Window' (small aluminium foil strips designed to act as radar reflectors and so confuse the enemy's radar picture). It was an incredibly successful tactic and one that reduced bomber losses for a number of raids, although the Germans soon developed tactics that lessened, but never negated, the use of this simple and cheap counter-measure. The Main Force consisted of 791 bombers, including 354 Lancasters from 19 Squadrons (four of these being Pathfinder units), with 103 Squadron sending no less than 27 aircraft (although three of these returned early and three were lost). This series

as we brought down the two-engined ones, and the destruction of four-engined bombers constitutes a much greater loss to the enemy." The four-engined bombers continued to increase in numbers, as did their striking power when Lancaster IIs were modified to carry an 8,000lb (3,600kg) bomb.

Following the Allied Commanders' Quebec conference in August, a new Directive was issued giving the bombers new priorities in the air build-up for the planned invasion of Europe. Many of the existing industrial targets were still included but there was to be increasing

January 1943, Lancaster II with four Bristol Hercules VI engines. DS604 served with 61 and 115 Squadrons before being lost on the Frankfurt operation of April 11, 1943. (FP Collection)

raid. Meanwhile the real Main Force attack by 711 aircraft was over Hanover. New countermeasures were being introduced at regular intervals; on October 8/9 the RCM Lancasters of 101 Squadron operated with ABC (Airborne Cigar) for the first time. The electronic war had become so complex and intense that on November 23 the RAF created No 100 Gp to specialise in RCM.

Battle of Berlin

November also saw the opening of what has been called the Battle of Berlin. The first raid took place on November 18/19 when 400 Lancasters attacked the 'Big City', with a second force attacking Ludwigshaven to split the night fighter force. A combination of poor weather and poor PFF marking led to a scattered raid — although losses were light. The night of November 22/23 saw the Command mount a maximum effort against Berlin; of the 765 bombers, 469 were Lancasters. Marking was accurate and Berlin was hit hard. An all-Lancaster force returned the following night, bombing through cloud. A few nights later, the 26/27th, it was again an all-Lancaster attack, by 443 aircraft, the mission marking the operational debut for another three 'Lanc' squadrons (432, 463 and 550), and results were again good; disaster, however, struck when the bombers returned to England. Virtually all the bases south of Yorkshire were covered in thick fog and as many aircraft were short of fuel they could not divert but had to try to land at bases in the south; a number of Lancasters crashed or crash-landed and a number of crewmen were killed. To complete what had been a bad night for the Lancaster force, 28 of the bombers that took part in the diversionary raid to Stuttgart were shot down.

December 2/3 was another dismal night for the Command; a planned maximum effort was abandoned when the Yorkshire-based Halifax units were fogged in. Other bombers turned back in bad weather over the North Sea. Results were poor and losses were once again high.

The start of the night attack on the Le Creusot steel works on June 19/20; bombs (left) are falling towards the Armament and Locomotive sections. (Ken Delve Collection)

of four major attacks on Hamburg caused major destruction in the city and seriously disrupted its war industries.

The series of Bomber Command attacks in late summer 1943 had proved the potential accuracy and destructive capability of the RAF's main strike weapon. German leaders had mixed reactions: in late August, Milch said, "[we] must decide on our priorities ... only the [Me] 110 in sufficient numbers can give us the necessary relief at night ... Germany is the real front line and the mass of fighters must go for home defence ... the only chance to defeat the day and night bombers"; whereas Jeschonnek (Chief of General Staff of the Luftwaffe) was of a different opinion: "Every four-engined bomber the Western Allies build makes me happy, for we will bring these down just

emphasis on lines of communication and the enemy air assets.

During the summer the loss rates of Stirlings and Halifaxes had once more raised questions at Bomber Command; the Stirlings on occasion suffering a staggering 16% loss rate. The Lancasters were not immune from losses and against targets such as Berlin were losing an average of just over 4%. The main problem was that of night fighters; once a fighter had located the bomber stream he was invariably able to find a number of targets — and multiple kills were becoming increasingly common.

One new tactic introduced in September was that of a 'spoof' raid — the first example was carried out by 21 Lancasters and eight Mosquitoes on the night of the 22nd/23rd on Oldenburg, with the pattern of the attack designed to simulate that of a Main Force

No 550 Sqn
"Per ignem vincimus" (Through fire we conquer)
Marks: I, III
Dates: Oct 1943 - Oct 1945
Group: 1 Gp
Bases: Waltham, North Killingholme
First Raid: Nov 26/27, 1943
Operational Losses:59
Unit Code: BQ

No 576 Sqn
"Carpe diem" (Seize the opportunity)
Marks: I, III
Dates: Nov 1943 - Sep 1945
Group: 1 Gp
Bases: Elsham Wolds, Fiskerton
First Raid: Nov 26/27, 1943 (Berlin)
Operational Losses:66
Unit Code: UL

No 582 Sqn
"Praecolamus designantes" (We fly before marking)
Marks: I, III
Dates: Apr 1944 - Sep 1945
Group: 8 (PFF) Gp
Base: Little Staughton
First Raid: Apr 9/10, 1944 (Lille)
Operational Losses:28
Unit Code: 6O (as in letter)
Victoria Cross: Capt E E Swales DFC SAAF
(pilot) [posthumous]

No 617 Sqn
"Apres moi le deluge" (After me the flood)
Marks: I, I (Special), III, VII
Dates: Mar 1943 - Sep 1946
Group: 5 Gp
Bases: Scampton, Coningsby, Woodhall
Spa, Waddington, Digri (India),
Binbrook
First Raid: May 16/17, 1943 (Mohne, Eder
& Sorpe Dams)
Operational Losses:32
Unit Codes: AJ, KC, YZ (Mk I [Specials])
Victoria Crosses: Wg Cdr G P Gibson DSO, DFC
(pilot), Wg Cdr G L Cheshire
DSO, DFC (pilot)

No 619 Sqn
no badge or motto
Marks: I, III
Dates: Apr 1943 - Jul 1945
Group: 5 Gp
Bases: Woodhall Spa, Coningsby,
Dunholme Lodge, Strubby, Skellingthorpe
First Raid: Jun 11/12, 1943 (Düsseldorf)
Operational Losses:77
Unit Code: PG

No 622 Sqn
"Bellamus noctu" (We make war by night)
Marks: I, III
Dates: Dec 1943 - Aug 1945
Group: 3 Gp
Bases: Mildenhall
First Raid: Jan 14/15, 1944
Operational Losses:44
Unit Code: GI

No 625 Sqn
"We avenge"
Marks: I, III
Dates: Oct 1943 - Oct 1945
Group: 1 Gp
Bases: Kelstern, Scampton
First Raid: Oct 18/19, 1945
Operational Losses:66
Unit Code: CF

Not all losses were to enemy action; this 97 Sqn aircraft was destroyed after a photo flash exploded. (Ken Delve Collection)

In a letter dated December 7, Harris outlined the recent achievements of his Command and concluded that, by April 1944, his Command could achieve "a state of devastation in which surrender is inevitable." This, however, he said, would require priority in production for Lancasters and equipment to make No 100 Gp fully operational.

Phase II of the Battle of Berlin began on December 16/17 and just under 500 bombers attacked Berlin (483 Lancasters) — but a combination of strong defences and bad weather on return to the UK meant that 54 aircraft were lost. A maximum effort, 700+ aircraft, attacked Berlin on December 29/30 and this was followed two nights later by an all-Lancaster raid. Lancasters were over Berlin again the next night but once more the enemy fighters proved effective — almost one third of the Pathfinders were lost or returned to base early. This ended Phase II; the assessment was that the Battle was proving harder than expected, partly because of the lower number of available aircraft (and thus bomb tonnage) following the decision to withdraw the Halifax from the Battle

— a decision that was reversed for the remaining two phases.

January 20/21 saw 769 bombers tasked to attack Berlin — little had changed from the previous attacks, results were at best average and losses were high (22 of the 35 lost aircraft being Halifaxes, out of a despatched force of 264 aircraft). The next raid, January 27/28 saw 515 Lancasters en route to Berlin; they made a reasonably effective attack but lost 33 of their number.

A maximum effort went out the following night, 432 'Lancs' being included in the 677 aircraft force. Berlin was hit again two nights later; with bomber losses still high, this brought Phase III to a close.

Despite the loss rates, this series of four attacks was assessed as a success and damage to Berlin was becoming significant.

The final Phase of the Battle comprised only two raids — on February 15/16 and March 24/25, 1944. On the second of these the overall loss rate was almost 10% — the highest of the campaign so far. Since November 18/19, 1943, the Command had mounted 9,099 sorties against Berlin (7,249 by Lancasters), dropping 29,804 tons of

A posed shot of 44 Squadron crews 'studying the map' prior to boarding their aircraft. (Ken Delve Collection)

bombs; overall losses were 501 aircraft, 380 of these being Lancasters.

Invasion of Europe

March saw the 'heavies' tasked against selected railway marshalling yards in France, the first of this sequence of eight attacks taking place on March 6/7 when Trappes was hit. These raids were connected with the initial parts of the pre-Overlord strategic bombing plan and although Bomber Command was still free to pursue its own strategic plan against German cities it would, from May,

Night after night the heavy bombers of Bomber Command attacked targets in Germany; by mid-1944 the bulk of this force was composed of Lancasters — painting by Michael Turner.

become increasingly involved on pre-invasion targets.

However, on the night of March 30/31 the major industrial city and communications interchange of Nuremberg was chosen for a Main Force attack and 795 bombers (572 Lancasters) left their bases in England. It was to be a disaster for Bomber Command with 95 aircraft (64 Lancasters) failing to return home. It started to go wrong from the moment the bomber stream penetrated German-held territory and the night fighters found the first of their prey. Les Bartlett was the Bomb Aimer in a 50 Squadron Lancaster out of Skellingthorpe: "We altered course for Nuremberg and I looked down at the area over which we had just passed. It looked like a battlefield. There were kites burning on the deck all over the place — bombs going off where they had been jettisoned by bombers damaged in combat, and fires from their incendiaries across the whole area. Such a picture of aerial disaster I had never seen before and hoped never to see again.

"On the way into the target the winds

became changeable and we almost ran into the defences of Schweinfurt — but we altered course in time. The defences of Nuremberg were nothing to speak of, a modest amount of heavy flak which did not prevent us doing a normal approach, and we were able to get the Target Indicators dropped by the Pathfinder Force in our bombsight and to score direct hits with our 4,000lb 'Cookie' and our 1,000lb bombs and incendiaries. We were able to get out of the target area, always a dodgy business, and set course for home. To reach the coast was a binding two-hour stooge. The varying

winds were leading us a dance. We found ourselves approaching Calais instead of being 80 miles further south, so we had a slight detour to avoid the defences. Once near the enemy coast, it was nose down for home at 300kts. Even then we saw some poor blokes 'buy it' over the Channel. What a relief it was to be flying over Lincoln Cathedral once more." The overall Lancaster loss rate, including five aircraft damaged beyond repair, was 12.1% — by far the worst total the type ever suffered (the Halifax force that night suffered a 16.8% loss rate).

The weather was partly to blame for scattering aircraft and putting them over defensive zones that should have been avoided; the majority of losses were, however, to night fighters.

Operational control of Bomber Command passed to SHAEF (Supreme HQ Allied Expeditionary Force) on April 14 and for the next three months the majority of effort was expended in direct or indirect support of the ground offensive. For the heavy

No 630 Sqn
"Nocturna mors" (Death by night)

Marks:	I, III
Dates:	Nov 1943 - Jul 1945
Group:	5 Gp
Base:	East Kirkby
First Raid:	Nov 18/19, 1943 (Berlin)
Operational Losses:	59
Unit Code:	LE

No 635 Sqn
"Nos ducimus ceteri secunter" (We lead others follow)

Marks:	I, III, VI
Dates:	Mar 1944 - Sep 1945
Group:	8 (PFF) Gp
Base:	Downham Market
First Raid:	Mar 22/23, 1944 (Frankfurt)
Operational Losses:	34
Unit Code:	F2
Victoria Cross:	Sqn Ldr I W Bazalgette DFC (pilot) [posthumous]

* = wartime Group only listed

COASTAL COMMAND, OVERSEAS & MISCELLANEOUS SQUADRONS

No 18 Sqn
"Animo et fide" (With courage and faith)

Marks:	GR 3
Dates:	Sep 1946 only
Command/Area:	Middle East
Role:	Maritime Reconnaissance
Base:	Ein Shemer (Palestine)
Unit Code:	none

No 37 Sqn
"Wise without eyes"

Marks:	III; VII; GR 3
Dates:	Apr 1946 - Aug 1953
Command/Area:	Mediterranean, Middle East
Role:	Maritime Reconnaissance
Bases:	Fayid (Egypt), Shallufa (Egypt), Ein Shemer (Palestine), Luqa (Malta)
Unit Code:	none

No 38 Sqn
"Ante lucem" (Before the dawn)

Marks:	ASR 3, GR 3
Dates:	Jul 1946 - Dec 1953
Command/Area:	Mediterranean, Middle East
Role:	Maritime Reconnaissance
Bases:	Luqa (Malta), Ein Shemer (Palestine), Shallufa (Egypt), Ramat David (Palestine)
Unit Code:	RL

No 40 Sqn
"Hostem coelo expellere"
(To drive the enemy from the sky)

Mark:	B VII
Dates:	Jan 1946 - Apr 1947
Command/Area:	Middle East
Role:	Heavy bomber
Bases:	Abu Sueir (Egypt), Shallufa (Egypt)
Unit Code:	BL

No 70 Sqn
"Usquam" (Anywhere)

Mark:	I
Dates:	Apr 1946 - Apr 1947
Command/Area:	Middle East
Role:	Heavy Bomber
Bases:	Fayid (Egypt), Kabrit (Egypt), Shallufa (Egypt)
Unit Code:	none

No 82 Sqn
"Super omnia ubique" (Over all things everywhere)
Mark: PR 1
Dates: Oct 1946 - Dec 1953
Command/Area: Bomber
Role: Photo-survey
Bases: Benson, Leuchars, Eastleigh (Kenya), Takoradi (Gold Coast), Wyton
Unit Code: none

No 104 Sqn
"Strike hard"
Mark: B VII
Dates: Nov 1945 - Apr 1947
Command/Area: Middle East
Role: Heavy Bomber
Bases: Abu Sueir (Egypt), Shallufa (Egypt)

No 120 Sqn
"Endurance"
Mark: GR 3
Dates: Nov 1946 - Apr 1951
Command/Area: Coastal
Role: Maritime Reconnaissance
Bases: Leuchars, Kinloss
Unit Code: BS

No 160 Sqn
"Api soya paragasamu" (We seek and strike)
Mark: GR III
Dates: Aug - Sep 1946
Command/Area: Coastal
Role: Maritime Reconnaissance
Base: Leuchars
Unit Code: BS

No 178 Sqn
"Irae emissarii" (Emissaries of wrath)
Mark: III
Dates: Nov 1945 - Apr 1946
Command/Area: Middle East
Role: Heavy Bomber
Base: Fayid (Egypt)
Unit Code: none

No 179 Sqn
"Delentem deleo" (I destroy the destroyer)
Mark: ASR III
Dates: Feb - Sep 1946
Command/Area: Coastal:
Role: Maritime Reconnaissance
Base: St Eval
Unit Code: OZ

No 203 Sqn
"Occidens oriensque" (West and East)
Marks: GR 3, ASR 3
Dates: Aug 1946 - Mar 1953
Command/Area: Coastal
Role: Maritime Reconnaissance
Bases: Leuchars, St Eval, St Mawgan, Topcliffe
Unit Code: CJ

No 210 Sqn
"Yn y nwyfre yn hedfan" (Hovering in the heavens)
Marks: GR 3, ASR 3
Dates: Jun 1946 - Oct 1952
Command/Area: Coastal
Role: Maritime Reconnaissance
Bases: St Eval, St Mawgan, Topcliffe
Unit Code: OZ

No 224 Sqn
"Fedele all'amico" (Faithful to a friend)
Marks: GR 3
Dates: Oct 1946 - Nov 1947
Command/Area: Coastal
Role: Maritime Reconnaissance
Base: St Eval
Unit Code: XB

Bombing up Lancaster I DV280 of 463 Squadron at Waddington. (Andy Thomas Collection)

bombers the most important targets were rail communications, the idea being to isolate the invasion area and prevent the Germans from moving reinforcements to Normandy. As D-Day approached, the bombers were tasked against other targets such as coastal defences. The heavy bomber force was committed to support operations in the hours leading up to the actual landings and a number of units had a highly specialised role to play in the deceptions campaign. Under Operations 'Taxable' and 'Glimmer', bombers, including 617 Squadron Lancasters, flew carefully-planned race-track patterns dropping 'window' to simulate the approach of a large naval force.

During the first week after D-Day (June 6, 1944) the Command flew over 2,500 sorties in support of the landings, attacking road and rail communications and a range of other targets. June 14 marked Bomber Command's return to daylight operations when 200 Lancasters attacked German naval targets threatening the invasion supply

lines. A great deal of effort was also being expended against V-weapon targets. The first of the V-1 rockets had fallen on England on June 6 and the destruction of construction, storage and launch sites became a high priority — and yet another diversion from the strategic offensive against the German homeland.

With a massively powerful day and night bomber force at their disposal, the Allied commanders looked at ways that this could prove a decisive weapon — and promptly disagreed as to its most effective employment. In essence this split into the supporters of the Transportation Plan and those of the Oil Plan; the former believed that the German economy and military could be 'strangled' through the destruction of its communication network, and especially rail communications; whilst the latter believed that oil was the weak link.

Not everyone in Bomber Command was happy with the employment of the Pathfinder Force and for some time No 5 Gp, under Air

Methwold and PB509 of 149 Squadron — with impressive nose art — fires up her engines; the aircraft served with 149 and 186 Squadrons before going to 1659 HCU. It survived the war and was struck off charge in December 1945. (Andy Thomas Collection)

Marshal Ralph Cochrane, had been developing its own techniques — in large measure prompted and led by distinguished bomber figures such as Guy Gibson and Leonard Cheshire. No 5 Gp had been the first of the all-Lancaster Groups and as such had developed the tactical employment of the type on both special and Main Force operations. Harris later summed up the situation as it stood in mid 1944: "No 5 Group operated largely as an independent unit and developed its own techniques, including the original Master Bomber concept, also offset skymarking continued to be developed e.g. '5 Gp Newhaven' using offset techniques 1-2,000 yards from the aiming point, any error in the Red TIs being cancelled by yellows from the Master Bomber. Other techniques developed, including 'sector bombing' with each aircraft given a heading and overshoot setting. This gave a good bomb distribution but needed very accurate low-level marking."

For much of the war Prime Minister Winston Churchill had what verged on paranoia regarding German Capital ships, and enormous bomber effort had been expended against such targets — with little result. In September 1944 the Admiralty believed that the battleship Tirpitz was about to leave the Kaa Fjord in Norway. The destruction of this battleship thus became a high priority and the Lancasters of 9 Squadron and 617 Squadron were tasked to attack the ship using 12,000lb (5,400kg) 'Tallboy' bombs. However, with these bombs aboard, the Lancasters were unable to reach the Kaa Fjord and return to their bases in England. The Russians were persuaded to accept the Lancasters at Yagodonik airfield near Archangel. Operation 'Paravane' called for the Lancasters to take off from Scotland, attack the Tirpitz and then land in Russia; Wg Cdr Willie Tait would lead 617 Squadron and Wg Cdr James Bazin would lead 9 Squadron. This plan was cancelled, and on September 11 the Lancasters flew direct to Yagodonik, the intention being to fly the attack from there. Weather conditions over Russia were poor and six of the Lancasters had to make forced-landings, the others being scattered over various airfields in Russia. Fg Off Ross was one of those who had to force-land.

"We had been circling for 2 hours 45 minutes, so I looked for a likely spot to land the aircraft, the surrounding ground appeared to be waterlogged. Finally, I selected a long stretch of wooden road, void of telegraph poles for a distance of about 1,100 yards. The cloud base was 200ft in patches and two approaches were made. The first was too far to the right, the second was OK, but a lorry load of troops had stopped on it. I tried the reciprocal without success. The Engineer reported about 30 gallons of petrol left, so I ordered the crew to crash stations, selected a marshy area, 20 degrees flap, and approached at 115 mph. Aircraft touched down, the crew were all OK."

The first task now was to gather as many of the serviceable aircraft as possible at Yagodonik; the final attack force of 28 Lancasters took off on September 28 led by Tait. Twenty-one aircraft carried 'Tallboys' and the others had 500lb 'Johnny Walker' mines. The attackers found the Tirpitz and made their runs, some having to go around twice due to bomb release trouble or poor line-ups. Seventeen of the 'Tallboys' were dropped and all the 500lb (227kg) mines — although an effective smoke screen had been thrown around the ship. No significant opposition had been encountered and all the Lancasters made it back to Yagodonik. There were conflicting reports as to the

Lancaster production was soon in full swing and aircraft came off the production line in large numbers; eventually, just over 7,000 aircraft were built in the UK and Canada. (FP Collection)

damage caused to the targets; although one bomb may have caused some damage, the Tirpitz was still afloat and was thus considered to be a threat. The Lancasters returned to the UK and the Germans moved the Tirpitz to the Tromso Fjord to act as a gun battery — a fact not known by the Admiralty. The move south had brought the ship in range of Lancasters flown from Scotland and on October 29, Tait led 40 aircraft (20 from each squadron) from Lossiemouth to attack the ship. Of the 32 'Tallboys' dropped, none caused any significant damage; one Lancaster was hit by flak but managed to land in Sweden. The third attack was mounted on November 12, Tait leading 31 bombers (18 from 617 Squadron and 13 from 9 Squadron). Good weather, no smoke screen and no fighters allowed the Lancasters to make accurate attacks and several hits were scored; the Tirpitz exploded and turned over. One Lancaster was damaged but landed in Sweden.

No 231 Sqn
no badge/motto

Mark:	III
Dates:	Dec 1945 - Jan 1946
Command/Area:	Transport
Role:	Transport
Base:	Full Sutton
Unit Code:	none

No 279 Sqn
"To see and be seen"

Mark:	ASR III
Dates:	Sep 1945 - Mar 1946
Command/Area:	Coastal
Role:	Air-Sea Rescue
Base:	Beccles
Unit Code:	RL

No 541 Sqn
"Alone above all"

Mark:	PR 1
Dates:	Jun - Sep 1946
Command/Area:	Bomber
Role:	Photo-survey
Base:	Benson
Unit Code:	none on Lancasters

No 621 Sqn
"Ever ready to strike"

Mark:	ASR III
Dates:	Apr - Sep 1946
Command/Area:	Middle East
Role:	Maritime Reconnaissance
Bases:	Aqir (Palestine), Ein Shemer (Palestine)
Unit Code:	none

No 683 Sqn
"Nihil nos later" (Nothing remains concealed)

Mark:	PR 1
Dates:	Nov 1950 - Nov 1953
Command/Area:	Middle East
Role:	Photo-survey
Bases:	Fayid (Egypt), Kabrit (Egypt), Eastleigh (Kenya), Khormaksar (Aden), Habbaniya (Iraq)
Unit Code:	none

Lancasters were employed on a range of other tasks postwar — as evidenced here with an ASR III equipped with airborne lifeboat. (FP Collection)

Although command of the bomber force reverted to the Air Staff on September 14, one of the first series of major operations was in support of the airborne landings in Holland as part of Operation 'Market-Garden'. The striking power of Bomber Command is aptly demonstrated by statistics for October 1944 — 17,000 operational sorties were flown, 13,000 of these to targets in Germany, and over 50,000 tons of bombs fell on German territory; in one 24-hour period the Command dropped more tonnage of bombs on Duisburg than the Germans dropped on London in the entire war.

October 14 opened Operation 'Hurricane' — the USAAF was to attack targets in the Ruhr by day and Bomber Command was to attack them by night — the intention being to demonstrate the Allies' overwhelming air power. For many crews this entailed flying on consecutive missions in the same 24-hour period, as 'maximum effort' was to be standard. On the first raid, 1,000+ RAF bombers hit Duisburg, crews landed back in England and in many cases snatched a few hours rest before taking off on the night attack.

The Lancasters of 150 Squadron were using Rose tail turrets in October; the turret carried two .5in guns rather than the standard four .303in guns and was part of Bomber Command's attempts to improve the

defensive fire-power of its bombers.

In his 'Despatches' Harris summarised these 1944 developments: "Air Ministry informed me that the provision of four-gun mid-upper turrets for Stirling, Halifax and Lancaster was being pushed ahead, but they would not be available for use by Bomber Command before August 1943. It was also stated that the introduction of two 20mm guns into the dorsal turret of Lancaster aircraft would not be feasible because of Centre of Gravity considerations.... owing to the lack of progress in the design of tail turrets with .5in guns, I directly encouraged Messrs Rose Bros of Gainsborough, who, with the assistance of Bomber Command personnel, designed and produced a tail turret carrying two .5in guns. This turret possessed novel features ... [and] provided a large field of view, since the rear portion of the cupola was left open as a direct vision opening." (By the end of the war 180 of these turrets had been installed in Lancasters of No 100 Gp.)

This was not, however, the first new gunnery system to enter operational use in 1944; in mid-July 460 Squadron began to fly with AGLT (Automatic Gun Laying Turret) fitted. As early as late October 1942, the TRE (Telecommuncations Research Establishment) had demonstrated a rearward-facing AI device that could be used as a blindfire aid

for the rear guns. An order was placed for 100 modified sets to be fitted to FN120 turrets (as FN121). Meanwhile, the BDU was undertaking intensive trials on the prototype AGLT in one of its Lancasters and although a few teething problems had to be overcome they were, in general terms, satisfied with the equipment. The first modified aircraft went to 460 Squadron in March and after a period of work-up, the Squadron flew its first mission on July 20/21.

By January 1945 the Command included 51 Lancaster squadrons in its front-line — a total established strength of around 1,200 aircraft; the remaining 50 or so squadrons were, primarily, equipped with the Halifax and Mosquito and some of the Halifax units would soon receive Lancasters.

In these latter months of the war the Lancaster once more proved its adaptability and the BI (Spec) was modified to take a 22,000lb (9,980kg) 'Grand Slam' bomb — another special weapon from the design genius of Barnes Wallis. Trials took place in February and the first production aircraft was PB995; the first two aircraft joined 617 Squadron on March 14 and that same afternoon one 'Lanc' (PD112 flown by Sqn Ldr C Calder joined the attack on the Bielefeld viaduct). Calder dropped his 'Grand Slam' from 14,000ft (4,270m) and scored a near miss (30 yards) which collapsed

Postwar, Lancaster BVII NX683 of 40 Squadron in white and black scheme over Egypt. (Andy Thomas Collection)

Whilst Lancaster ND513 taxies in, another of 207 Squadron's aircraft lands with its starboard outer engine on fire — painting by Michael Turner.

two of the arches of the viaduct. 'Tallboys' dropped by other Lancasters caused further damage. The Lancasters were next tasked to destroy the Arnsberg viaduct but the attack of March 15 was aborted for weather; the following day six 'Grand Slam' and 13 'Tallboy' aircraft returned to this target — all dropped within 200 yards and the viaduct was destroyed. In the second half of the month other bridge targets were destroyed by these awesome weapons.

The last major raid of the war took place on April 25 when 375 Lancasters (and Mosquitos) attacked the Berghof (Hitler's 'Eagle's Nest' chalet) and the associated SS barracks at Berchtesgaden in the Bavarian Alps.

The next major task for the bombers was a far more peaceful one — the dropping of food supplies to the hard-pressed population of Holland. Operation 'Manna' commenced on April 28, the first sorties being flown by Lancasters of 115 Squadron. In a two-week period the Command flew 3,000 sorties and dropped 7,000 tons of food.

The war with Germany ended on May 8, but even before that a massive repatriation plan was under way. As part of Operation 'Exodus', aircraft were used to fly ex-PoWs back to England and a number of Lancasters were converted to carry 25 passengers. The first 'Exodus' sortie was flown out of Brussels on May 4; during the month 3,000 such sorties were flown and 74,000 PoWs flown home. A similar operation was mounted, Operation 'Dodge', to bring the troops home from Italy and the Central Mediterranean.

Tiger Force

The war with Japan was, however, still fierce and although the Allies were inexorably advancing towards Japan itself, there was still a great deal yet to do. Part of the planned build-up of air power was the creation of Tiger Force, making use of squadrons no longer needed for the war in Europe. Amongst the units earmarked for Tiger Force were three bomber groups, each comprising ten Lancaster squadrons. The designated squadrons were equipped with the Lancaster I (FE) - for Far East - and Lancaster VII (FE) and undertook long-range training flights as part of their work-up. The aircraft themselves were given more appropriate camouflage schemes of white upper surfaces and black undersurfaces, along with various airframe and armament modifications, including additional fuel tankage that gave them a 3,000 mile range. The planned deployment date slipped from summer to autumn but the dropping of the atom bombs on Japan in early August brought the Far East war to an end and the Tiger Force deployment was cancelled on September 2.

World War Two was over and it was time to return to a peaceful footing as soon as possible — for economic and other reasons. The inevitable consequence was a rapid run-down of squadrons; within a matter of months almost 30 Lancaster squadrons had gone. Commonwealth and Allied units were released from RAF service and in many cases, especially that of the Canadian No 6 Gp, returned home with their aircraft.

Final words are best left to Sir Arthur Harris: "Suffice it to say that the Lancaster, measured in no matter what terms, was, and still is, incomparably the most efficient. In range, bomb carrying capacity, ease of handling, freedom from accident, and particularly in casualty rate, it far surpassed the other heavy types. Hence the constant pressure brought by HQ Bomber Command for concentration on Lancaster production at the expense of other types, and hence the policy to employ every available Lancaster in the front line, even at the expense of an uneconomical training set-up."

Re-sparring PA474

Surrounded by a mass of ladders and trestles, PA474 looked somewhat like a beached whale as she was taken apart. (FP - Steve Fletcher)

During the winter of 1995/96 the Battle of Britain Memorial Flight's Avro Lancaster PA474 underwent a major wing re-spar programme. Robert Rudhall monitored the daunting task from beginning to end.

IT WAS something which had never been attempted before, but it had to be done if Avro Lancaster B.I PA474 was to continue in its role as a flying tribute to Britain's aviation heritage. Nobody had ever re-sparred a Lancaster bomber — the aircraft was expected to have a relatively short lifespan during World War Two so there was simply no need to even think about fitting a replacement wing spar.

Since 1976 PA474 has been the flagship of the RAF's Battle of Britain Memorial Flight (BBMF), appearing at countless events all over the UK and sometimes venturing into Europe. The 'Bomber', as it is known at the BBMF, is very much a working aircraft and averages between 85 and 100 flying hours during each display season, which normally runs from late April through to the end of September.

Every aircraft has a finite fatigue life, so in order to keep a close check on the airframe's integrity, monitoring equipment was fitted to PA474 when she joined BBMF. Fatigue meter readings showed that by the end of December 1983 the aircraft had flown for 3,060 hours, and that there were around 1,340 hours (or 12 years, based on the current usage) left before major airframe work would be necessary to keep the 'Bomber' flying.

At the end of the 1995 flying season PA474 had virtually used up its airframe fatigue life, but the debate over what to do when this cut-off point was reached had been going on for years. It was obvious that the Lancaster was a very emotive subject — the lobby for keeping her airworthy for as long as possible would be very strong indeed. Any talk of permanently grounding the aircraft would be certain to incense many thousands of veterans and aircraft enthusiasts.

To explain something of the genesis of the Lancaster's re-spar work it is necessary to go back to another four-engined RAF aircraft, the bulbous-nosed Armstrong-Whitworth Argosy. During the transport's career with the air force it was found that cracks were developing in the top spar booms. Because there were similarities

between the Argosy's wing construction and that of the Avro Shackleton, an instruction was issued to inspect all of the remaining Shackletons in RAF service. As a result, it was noticed that some of the bolt holes in the Shackleton's spar booms nearly intersected, which weakened the boom and in turn increased the risk of fatigue failure.

With the testing of the Shackleton spars completed it was decided that it might be a good idea to inspect the Lancaster's spars, and after deliberation, plans were put in hand to re-work the 'Lanc' at the end of the current spar's fatigue life, in late 1995.

This in turn posed the next major question in the equation — was there sufficient material to build the required new spars? Luckily metal extrusions left over from the Shackleton re-spar programme some years earlier had been saved and could be made available. Then it was necessary to ask, who would carry out the work?

The plan to re-spar the 'Lanc' had been in force at British Aerospace (BAe) since 1990. BAe, which holds the design authority for the Avro Type 683 Lancaster, was asked to define the work needed to replace the spars.

By the end of 1993 the new spar booms had

the stalwart hero

been manufactured from the raw metal billets, so that when the time came, there would be no delays — then in July 1995 BAe Aerostructures at Chadderton, near Manchester, accepted the contract to carry out the work on PA474.

On September 25, with the display season over, the Lancaster left its Coningsby base bound for RAF St Athan in Wales. As the 'Bomber' approached Wales the weather conditions worsened and plans to carry out flypasts over some local towns had to be abandoned. After landing, the aircraft was towed inside one of St Athan's large hangars. PA474 would spend the next eight months in various stages of disassembly, while major surgery was performed on its airframe.

Squadron Leader Frank Lovejoy was appointed as Project Officer for the work at St Athan and his right-hand man was Chief Technician Phil Royle. Phil was no stranger to the Lancaster, for he served as a Corporal on the engineering support team at BBMF from 1980 until 1984, and was one of the team members who conducted the major overhaul on the aircraft in 1993. Celebrating 21 years in the RAF during 1996, Phil was the ideal man to guide the team through the daunting task that lay ahead.

Around 25 RAF technicians from all over the UK were brought in to work on the 'Lanc'. Some came from as far away as RAF St Mawgan in Cornwall and others arrived from the opposite end of the country, namely RAF Kinloss in Scotland. RAF stations at Brize Norton, Marham and Wittering also supplied manpower for the job. With 'the team' gathered, the huge job could begin!

First of all, performance checks were carried out on each of the four Rolls-Royce Merlin engines prior to them being removed from the airframe. The resultant data, relating to everything from temperature

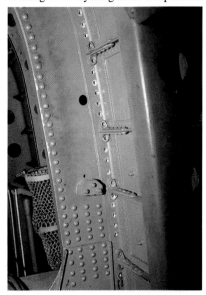

Inside the aircraft many hundreds of bolts had to be removed before the fuselage sections could be prised apart and the centre section made ready for transporting. (FP - Steve Fletcher)

The Lancaster at RAF St Athan on October 11, 1995. Up on trestles, all four engines have been removed along with the outer wings. (FP - Steve Fletcher)

and pressure to rpm would provide a comparison with that gathered when the overhauled Merlins were refitted. The Lancaster was then de-fuelled, after which a number of x-rays were taken of certain areas which are difficult to examine using conventional methods when the aircraft is in one piece. Especially critical were the fifth and eleventh ribs on the outer wings, for these are the aileron attachment points. The rudder hinge posts also came in for similar treatment.

The fuel tank panels were removed from the wings and at this point in the proceedings the tail was raised and the aircraft levelled out on jacks. The fuel tanks were then despatched to another part of St Athan for pressure testing.

The removal of the wing trailing edge closure panels was next on the agenda. As all of these are pop riveted to the airframe it took some time to remove them; especially as each of the rivets had to be drilled out.

Then it was time to remove the wheels and undercarriage. One of the undercarriage units was despatched to Dowty's at Cheltenham in Gloucestershire, where it was re-worked and re-sealed. This was followed by the removal of the four propellers and Merlin engines. One of the Merlins had been on the 'Lanc's' wing for 500 hours, during which time it performed perfectly — testament indeed to the high standards of maintenance employed by the BBMF. The Merlin engines were transported by road back up to RAF Coningsby where the Flight's engineers carried out winter maintenance. The four propellers were sent to Arrow Aviation near Exeter, Devon, for complete overhauls. Bit by bit the Lancaster was being 'scattered' all over the UK!

The next step was to remove the outer engine nacelles, followed by the bulkheads and subframes, after which it was the turn of the inboard wing trailing edges. The ailerons and flaps were then taken off — the Lancaster was getting smaller by the day.

The flaps were x-rayed, and apart from a few minor cracks, which were quite normal, they were found to be in very good condition for the age of the aircraft.

The Lancaster at this stage had to be trestled and lowered several feet so that it could be split down to its major components, ready for the arrival of the wings and centre section from Chadderton. This presented something of a problem, for where in the RAF of the 1990s do you acquire trestles to fit a Lancaster?

Chief Tech Phil Royle takes up the story: "We actually used modern-day RAF Tornado wing trestles and wheeled trolleys, but we had to modify them by taking the Tornado adapters off the top and replacing them

"The fact that the team were working on the RAF's last flying Lancaster bomber certainly galvanised people into action. "

with purpose-built wooden trestles. These items had to be made from scratch to exact specifications by our carpentry section here at RAF St Athan."

The fact that the team were working on the RAF's last flying Lancaster bomber certainly galvanised people into action. When requesting parts and specially-made items, from inside and outside the RAF, all the stops were pulled out to deliver whatever was required in double quick time!

Sgt Bryan Ascroft, one of the core engineering team, recalls: "At one stage we required some specially-made incidence boards to measure the incidence on the outer wing mainplane panels. We asked our carpentry section one evening for the boards, and normally a job like this would have taken about a week to come through the system. We actually had the fully made-up boards delivered to us the following afternoon!"

The aircraft's starboard outer wing assembly awaits packing and shipping off to Chadderton. (FP - Steve Fletcher)

With PA474 positioned on its trestles, the next major task was to take both outer wings away from the centre section. The panels where the outer wings join the centre section were the first to be removed, exposing the wing bolt attachment assemblies. When the aircraft was built in 1945 the wing bolts had been covered by a rubberised material to prevent any corrosion from penetrating the structure. This made the team's job that much easier and the wing bolts came away without too much fuss.

It was then time to remove the outer wings, but before this was carried out the team had to find out the weight of these components in order to arrange a suitable crane. But as that kind of information isn't readily available these days it was decided to play safe and base the weight calculations on the Shackleton's outer wings, as it was the nearest comparative aircraft type. The Shack's wings weigh 2,600lb (1,180kg) and a crane was arranged which could cope with that weight. As it transpired, the outer wings of the Lancaster weighed in at only 1,500lb (680kg), so the crane coped with the task admirably. Laying the outer wings on floor trestles, the team's attention then focused on the nose, centre section and rear fuselage.

To remove the nose from the centre section meant that all of the electrical wiring, hydraulic pipes and control runs had to be taken out of the airframe. Luckily, during an earlier overhaul the 'Lanc's' electrical wiring system had been renewed and in the process of doing so connecting plugs had been inserted at the areas of the 'fuselage breaks'. This meant that the wiring could all be 'unplugged' and rolled back into the respective parts of the airframe, which avoided having to cut any of the wiring or renew any of the looms, and saved a lot of time and money in the process.

Splitting the nose from the centre section was a long and painstaking job — a mind-numbing number of bolts had to be undone, bagged and labelled. The same operation was repeated on the control runs and hydraulic piping — none of which was

With the major components of the Lancaster now split asunder, the centre section was turned through 90° and hoisted onto a King trailer ready for the long road journey to BAe at Chadderton, near Manchester. Before any road trip could be contemplated, the route had to be surveyed by Chief Tech Fritz Williamson from the RAF's Aircraft Repair and Transportation Flight (AR&TF) and Phil Royle, plus a team from the AR&TF who had been tasked with moving the airframe. It would be their job to plan a route free of any obstacles such as low bridges, lamp posts, narrow traffic islands, etc.

In late October 1995 the centre section, outer wings and trailing edges, embarked upon the

Work was also carried out on some internal positions of the outer wings. Here a BAe engineer sits in the fuel tank bay while fitting new stringers to the starboard wing structure. (FP - Steve Fletcher)

particularly difficult, just very, very, time consuming!

During the disassembly and subsequent re-assembly process, the technical paperwork was being co-ordinated by Sgt Dick Chaffey. Dick joined the RAF in 1984 and was trained on the Hawker Hunter, so the technology of the Lancaster was not too alien to deal with. "Thankfully," said Dick, "we had access to around 10,000 drawings on microfilm which were made available from BBMF and BAe. It was this infrastructure which made the job a viable proposition. I'm particularly pleased with the way that the military worked in very close co-operation with BAe and various civilian contractors. This sort of working together attitude has never been experienced before and it worked really well. Mind you, when people know that they are helping to keep a Lancaster airworthy, national pride certainly comes into play."

The next major operation was to remove the rear fuselage from the centre section. Once the nose and rear fuselage had been disconnected they were carefully wheeled away from the rest of the airframe, splitting the 'Bomber' into three parts. A minor inspection was then conducted on the portions of the Lancaster which would be departing to BAe, so that any remedial work could be completed before the parts returned to St Athan ready for re-fitting to the rest of the airframe.

trip to BAe Chadderton. In the meantime, BAe had been busy constructing the purpose-built jigs, ready to accept the large chunks of Lancaster. The work that BAe would carry out included replacement of the rear spar upper boom, the spar web (the section of metal which joins the upper and lower spars giving the wing its inherent strength), and the lower centre section spar boom and web, plus renewal of all the attachment bolts. These components had already been constructed by BAe using microfilmed drawings, and were waiting as 'kits of parts'.

Colin Johnson, BAe Chadderton's Project Manager for the Military Business Unit, explains further: "The new material left over from the Shackleton spar programme was used to manufacture the new spars for the Lancaster, but we did not drill any holes in the new booms. This meant that the drilling and hole pattern could be copied from the Lancaster's existing spar booms. We cut the existing spar webs at the lower one third depth in order to give residual strength with one boom removed. On the outer wings, we only replaced the lower one third of the web adjacent to the boom. During this process we decided to replace all of the boom to web fasteners. This was necessary in case some of the original fasteners were oversized or damaged. In theory there was enough fatigue life remaining on the wing joint shackles, but it was considered prudent to replace these as well. The new spar booms which have been fitted to the aircraft have, in effect, a zero time fatigue life, so it will stand the aircraft in good stead for a long time to come."

I asked Colin how many hours were put into the project. "When we tendered for the job it was a fixed price contract, so we had to figure out how many man-hours it would involve. We had a 12-strong team working on the aircraft at any one time. There were four engineers working on the centre section during the day, and because this is the 'largest chunk' of the airframe, we also had a night shift. Three men completed all the remedial tasks on the outer wings, along with another team on the aircraft's wing trailing edges. Involvement in the Lancaster permeated its way throughout the whole factory as the inspection department and other areas at BAe came into contact with the project. Around 5,000 production hours were spent on the aircraft before it left the factory to go back to St Athan."

With the aircraft broken down into its major components, here was the ideal chance to inspect, clean and rectify any internal areas of the wings which needed attention, as well as to carry out a small amount of re-skinning. Some minor outbreaks of corrosion were easily and quickly dealt with, and on the whole the airframe was found to be in exceptional condition.

While the wings and centre section were at Chadderton, work forged ahead on the rest of the Lancaster at St Athan. Some maintenance was carried out on the remaining portions and, due to the nature of the bomber's disassembly, various areas were found to be in need of minor repairs. Some of the aircraft's flying control tubes, plus bearings and bearing housings were also

Up at British Aerospace Aerostructures, Chadderton, the Lancaster's wing centre section was put into a purpose-built jig, ready for the removal of the old spars and fitting of the newly made units. (FP - Steve Fletcher)

renewed. The mid-upper gun turret was removed from the rear fuselage, totally refurbished, new Perspex was fitted and the whole assembly was made ready to be refitted to the aircraft.

After much toil and sweat, not to mention endless hours of work at BAe Chadderton, the re-worked parts of PA474 were ready to make the return journey to St Athan. The centre section 'hit the road' during the last week in February 1996. In order to give the team at St Athan a chance to prepare and trestle the section, the starboard wing was not scheduled to arrive until March 12, with the port wing following around a week later. The next move was to get the newly-skinned areas of the wing repainted and carry out some additional work on the assemblies before the 'Bomber' could be put back together.

Slowly but surely the 'Lanc' started to take

shape once again, the nose section and rear fuselage were bolted back onto the centre section. And while this may sound like a simple procedure many hundreds of bolts had to be connected — a task which is made even more difficult by the cramped confines of the Lancaster's narrow fuselage.

As Phil Royle explains: "Once the additional work was completed and the front and back assemblies of the aircraft were re-fitted, the mounting of the wings happened fairly fast. We put the port wing back onto the centre section on March 20 and the starboard followed on March 25. The next major parts to go back together were the inner and outer wing trailing edges. Once we fitted those we carried out incidence checks to ensure that they were correctly aligned with the remainder of the wing mainplane. If they were incorrect then the aircraft would not fly properly or safely! Having

Back at RAF St Athan in March 1996 and 'The Bomber' is starting to take shape once again. Here the outer wings are back in position and the engineers are refitting the port inner engine bulkhead. (FP - Duncan Cubitt)

The 'old' spars. Looking like just ordinary strips of metal, these spars had been in the aircraft since she was built in 1945. They were subsequently cut up into small pieces and offered for sale by the Lincolnshire Lancaster Association, the civilian support organisation for the BBMF. (FP - Steve Fletcher)

satisfied ourselves that everything was OK, we refitted the ailerons and flaps.

"Running in parallel to this work was the re-assembly of the undercarriage assemblies. The fully-refurbished undercarriage 'leg' had returned from Dowty's, so in effect the Lancaster had one brand new leg fitted to it. After we put the legs back on we then raised the aircraft three feet on its trestles so that we could fit the wheels. The fuel tanks were then put back into their respective wing bays and we started to offer up the four Merlin engines to their bulkheads. Number three went on first and the other Merlins followed in a two, one and four order. After refitting the engines we had to carry out another incidence check to make sure that nothing had moved during the engine refitting process. We also did a symmetry check at the same time."

Bryan Ascroft, who normally works on VC.10s at RAF Brize Norton, was one of the engineers seconded onto the Lancaster project during the re-build. "When you are dealing with an aircraft like the Lancaster you have to go right back to your basic training," he remarked. "Things you are taught when you first join the RAF come into play again. We were really treading new ground with this work — after all, who has experience in offering up Lancaster wings to the aircraft's centre section these days? Just requesting parts could sometimes be a prolonged affair, for we had to quote the original part numbers to BAe who would tell us what the modern equivalent was. We then had to go to the RAF's Identification Cell at Wyton, who looked it up and told us if it was available and where we could get it from."

Thorough testing of the 're-plumbed'

hydraulics had to be completed, i.e. undercarriage retraction tests, correctly functioning bomb bay doors, the flaps were also checked at all their various increments. Once the systems were working perfectly, the aircraft's emergency nitrogen-based 'undercarriage blowdown' system had to be installed and tested. This is a back-up to the hydraulic system which can be used in an emergency to lower the wheels if the main system fails for any reason. Obviously it is imperative to make sure that the emergency system is functioning properly, just in case a problem should arise and the aircraft cannot lower its legs. After testing, the hydraulics had to be 'cleared out' so that no trace of the nitrogen was left in the pipes before re-introducing the standard fluid.

With the multitude of tests complete, the Lancaster was lowered to the ground for the first time in approximately six months. The aircraft was then fuelled and the various instruments were calibrated to make sure they were supplying the correct readings. However, before the Lancaster could be deemed fit for its first test flight, a series of engine runs and fuel flow tests had to be undertaken, along with compass swings, which could only take place on the airfield in winds of less than 5kts, as the aircraft has to be perfectly still to ensure correct alignment. This took some time to achieve, as it just happened (Sod's law) to coincide with a period of high winds in the St Athan area!

Time was marching on and it was obvious that the Lancaster would not be ready in time to fulfil some of its early 1996 display commitments, but as Phil Royle pointed out, "This job is a one-off, it's never been done before, and probably will never be done again. In terms of its scale, we put it akin to climbing Mount Everest, so in that respect it has got to be done properly. If that means the aircraft is delivered back to BBMF a little later than scheduled, then so be it. We are dealing with heritage with a capital H here

and we cannot afford to, and have no intention of, cutting corners."

The team at St Athan were very flexible in their working commitment to the Lancaster. Their average day started at 7.30am and usually did not end until 8pm — on many occasions it was even later than that! Where the aircraft and schedule demanded it, weekend work was duly undertaken.

With all of the requisite tests complete, the 'Lanc' actually emerged from the hangar some 69lbs (31kg) heavier than when she went in. This extra weight was a by-product of using modern bolts, screws and rivets to replace the older ones.

May 13 was the date fixed for the first air test. *FlyPast* Magazine had been following

"Arriving in the BBMF's Dakota, the 'Lanc' crew were obviously eager to get their hands back on their bomber."

the re-spar work closely and a representative from the publication was privileged to fly down with the Lancaster crew to St Athan to watch the test flight and accompany the bomber on the return journey home to Coningsby (the only aviation magazine to do so). Arriving in the BBMF's Dakota, the 'Lanc' crew were obviously eager to get their hands back on their bomber. As pilot Flt Lt Mike Chatterton drew closer to PA474, his affection for the aircraft spilled over into words... "There's my girl!".

Phil Royle explained to the crew exactly what had been done to the aircraft over the winter and then finally it was time to board the 'Bomber'. The crew comprised: Mike Chatterton (captain), Flt Lt Jerry Ward (co-pilot). Flt Lt Eric Deas (nav), Sgt Nick Wolfenden (eng), plus Sqn Ldr Dave Buchanan as observer. Dave was being trained up as an additional Lancaster display

In the foreground the starboard outer engine mounting assembly, framed by the aircraft's propellers, waits its turn to be refitted to PA474. (FP - Duncan Cubitt)

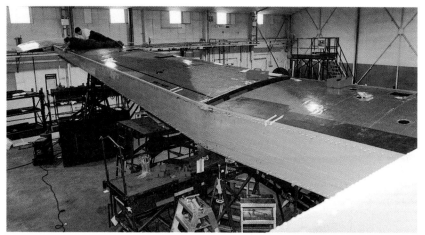

Two engineers perch precariously on the end of the Lancaster's port wing, making adjustments to hundreds of bolts, ready for the refitting of the wing's trailing edge. (FP - Duncan Cubitt)

The Lancaster's starboard undercarriage unit was totally reworked by Dowty's and was returned to the aircraft in mint condition. A Dowty representative and one of St Athan's engineers make final adjustments before fitting the wheel. (FP - Duncan Cubitt)

engine temperatures and pressures were then recorded and the fuel load used was determined. A number of minor snags were detected during the flight test and after the de-brief it was decided to leave the bomber at St Athan for another day so that Phil and his team could sort them out.

May 15 dawned and the 'Lanc' crew (along with *FlyPast's* representative) once again departed Coningsby to return PA474 back to Lincolnshire... 'Bomber County'. This time the trip to Wales was courtesy of an RAF Lyneham-based C-130 Hercules which was on a training sortie. The crew for PA474's return trip comprised: Mike Chatterton (captain), Jerry Ward (co-pilot), Sqn Ldr Brian Clark (nav), Nick Wolfenden (eng) and Master Engineer Nick Jones (second eng) — Nick was in his first season with BBMF and was there to see what the engineer's tasks are on the Lancaster. So, with five 'up front', the Lancaster's small cockpit was quite crowded!

The BBMF's engineers and groundcrew gave the bomber a once over as Phil Royle and his team detailed the work done since the air test two days before. Satisfied that the aircraft was in tip-top condition, Mike Chatterton accepted and signed the Lancaster's Form 700 from Sqn Ldr Frank Lovejoy and PA474 was officially handed back to BBMF.

As we all walked out from the crew room towards the four-engined bomber I was reminded of that scene in the 'The Dambusters', when Richard Todd as Guy Gibson says "Right, let's go!"... Everybody climbed aboard and strapped in for the flight back to Coningsby. It was planned that after take-off Mike would perform a few passes over RAF St Athan for the benefit of the assembled crowd — people had appeared from every nook and cranny on the airfield to wave the 'Lanc' goodbye.

With a fuel load of 650 Imp gallons (2,955 litres) on board, the four Merlins were started, then engine runs and magneto drop checks were performed — all was in order,

captain (he is now the BBMF's Bomber Leader), and was going along for the ride to watch the crew in action, as were some of the St Athan engineering team who had worked on the aircraft.

After starting up and carrying out a number of engine runs and systems tests, the Lancaster took off at 3.27pm on her first air test.

She climbed, initially to 7,000ft (2,130m), with the crew checking the airspeed indicator and altimeter throughout the climb. After a period at height, the aircraft was brought back down to 4,000ft (1,220m) where the 'services' (flaps, undercarriage, etc) were checked for operation and timings. Stall tests were then performed in 'clean' and 'dirty' configuration, with the bomber stalling in 'dirty' configuration at an amazing 45kts (51.7mph). Engine shut down and propeller feathering drills were also part of the test sequence.

Returning to St Athan at 4.37pm the 'Lanc' made a couple of passes over the personnel gathered below before landing —

The first take-off! PA474 lifts off from St Athan's main runway on May 13, 1996, for its first flight since being re-sparred. Pilots were F/L Mike Chatterton (Captain) and F/L Jerry Ward (Co-pilot). (FP - Robert Rudhall)

and we taxied out to the end of runway 08, ready for take-off.

At 2.25pm the engines were run up to take-off power, temperatures and pressures were checked, clearance was given from the control tower, and the black bomber rolled down the runway swiftly gathering speed until Mike Chatterton lifted her smoothly off the ground. "Undercarriage up, flaps up", and the large aircraft headed back for the first of several flypasts over St Athan. With one final fly-by down the main runway, Mike rocked the wings gently in a 'goodbye wave' to Wales and the bomber set course for Cowbridge and Maesteg, where flypasts were duly performed by Jerry Ward, in a salute to the many locals who had also worked on the aircraft during its stay in Wales.

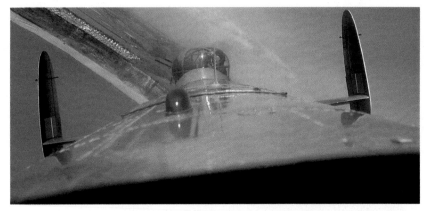

The 'Lanc' carries out a steep turn over the Welsh coastline during its return flight from St Athan to Coningsby on May 15, 1996. (FP - Robert Rudhall)

"After a low pass over Cardiff Airport we gained height and set course for RAF Coningsby in Lincolnshire."

After a low pass over Cardiff Airport we gained height and set course for RAF Coningsby in Lincolnshire. En route, another flypast was performed over Filton airfield, near Bristol, once home to the Bristol Aeroplane Company, but now operated by British Aerospace. Maintaining between 2,000ft (610m) and 3,000ft (914m) the bomber made its way up country, flying over the Cotswold towns of Cheltenham and Gloucester while under the guidance of Brize Norton radar, eventually passing over the British Aviation Heritage's airfield at Bruntingthorpe, Leics. Looking down on the former USAF facility you could be forgiven for thinking you were passing over an RAF airfield during the 1950s, for parked out on the hardstandings were a Vulcan, Victor, Hunters, Lightnings and Canberras.

Shortly after leaving the Bruntingthorpe area, the crew made radio contact with RAF Cottesmore near Stamford, which it just so happened was holding its bi-annual Tornado Meet. A request came from the tower for a flypast, and Mike duly obliged with a run at 300ft (91m) down the double line-up of Tornados. Banking away from Cottesmore, the 'Lanc' made her way on the final leg of the flight home.

Meanwhile, over at RAF Coningsby, a sizeable crowd had gathered at BBMF's base to welcome the flagship of the Flight — as we flew low over the BBMF's hangar, hundreds were waving to us from the airfield and the roadside. After several passes for the benefit of the local television and newspaper cameras, the undercarriage and flaps were lowered as we entered the downwind leg for landing.

Mike and Jerry made a textbook touchdown on runway 08 at 4.15pm. All too soon the flight was over and we were taxiing towards the dispersal area. Trundling around the airfield's perimeter track, the crew carried out a final post-flight check of the engines' rpms, temperatures and pressures before she came to a halt. The 'Bomber' was home.

This mammoth undertaking has ensured that PA474 will remain in an airworthy condition for a long time to come. The engineers involved — both military and civilian at St Athan and Chadderton — deserve full recognition for their dedication and quality of work. Once again, just like during World War Two, it was the unsung men and women on the ground who kept the Avro Lancaster in the air.

The author would like to thank the following for their help and co-operation during the re-sparring process: all at RAF St Athan, British Aerospace Aerostructures, Chadderton and the Battle of Britain Memorial Flight, RAF Coningsby.

Roaring low over RAF Coningsby, the 'Bomber' returns home on May 15, 1996. Its re-spar will enable it to remain in airworthy condition well into the next century! (FP - Robert Rudhall)

1..2..3...
GO FOR THE NEW
LOWE CATALOGUE

COMMUNICATIONS

AMATEUR RADIO

GPS NAVIGATION

SHORT WAVE LISTENING

AIRBAND RADIO

SCANNERS

WEATHER MONITORING

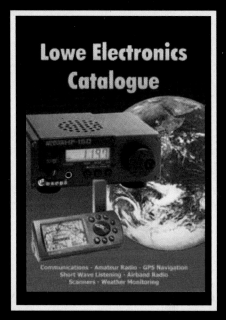

Over the last 20 years we have built a solid reputation with our customers for providing exciting and innovative products, backed up by the finest service and support expertise available anywhere in the UK. We have specialised in the sale of everything for the airband radio enthusiast, ranging from simple VHF only receivers to multiband scanners covering all civil, military and HF communications channels.We manufacture some of the best short wave receivers in the world, and also supply radio decoding software, ham radio equipment, weather monitoring station equipment and much, much more.We have just produced our first ever 80 page full colour mail order catalogue, and you now have the chance to receive this ABSOLUTELY FREE. With no obligation to purchase at all, we are confident that you will find one of the most comprehensive product offerings in this area of technology available anywhere in the world.We are also confident that you will find something there to interest

you. Just send four first class stamps to cover the postage to Lowe Electronics, and we will send our bumper colour catalogue by return.

LOWE ELECTRONICS LTD
Chesterfield Road
Matlock
Derbyshire DE4 5LE
Telephone 01629 580800
Fax 01629 580020
Email: info@lowe.co.uk
URL: http://www.lowe.co.uk

Displaying the 'Lanc'

The Battle of Britain Memorial Flight's Avro Lancaster PA474 averages between 85/100 hours flying time per year and delights the crowds wherever she goes. (FP - Duncan Cubitt)

Only two airworthy Avro Lancasters survive worldwide. Robert Rudhall talks to the current pilots of both aircraft about the intricacies of displaying their respective heavy bombers at airshows.

REAT BRITAIN AND Canada are currently the only two places in the world where you can see an Avro Lancaster bomber airborne. Both of these aircraft fly on a regular basis, delighting the thousands of people who relish the sound of four Rolls-Royce Merlin engines running in unison. And although the two Lancasters fly under the strictest of limitations and standards, they both have different operating procedures. FlyPast has had the honour of flying in PA474 and 'KB726', which of course provided a useful opportunity to observe both sets of crews 'in action'.

The UK-based Battle of Britain Memorial Flight's (BBMF) B.I PA474 is still a military-owned aircraft and as such has to comply with current RAF regulations. In contrast, the Canadian Warplane Heritage (CWH) Lancaster, B.X 'KB726' (C-GVRA), is a civilian-owned machine and therefore must abide by Canadian airworthiness requirements.

Though they operate at opposite ends of the spectrum, there appear to be few obvious differences between the two aircraft — until you look at the flightgear. PA474's crew all wear regulation RAF 'bonedome'-style helmets and oxygen masks, while the CWH crew utilise standard airline-style headsets and microphones. The latter may be the more comfortable to wear, but they were not really designed to cope with the high noise levels inside

The BBMF's PA474 always starts No 3 engine first to power up the generators and compressors. (FP - Robert Rudhall)

a Lancaster — as a result the crew often have to communicate by hand signals when voices are drowned out by the mighty Merlins.

'KB726' currently sits in the 'four-engined heavy' bracket of the Canadian Department of Transport's categorisation process, so in theory any civil pilot who currently flies four-engined airliners could legally climb into the cockpit and take the Lancaster 'for a spin'. Of course, that is never going to happen — not surprisingly, the CWH is very particular about who flies its

Lancaster. As with the RAF's PA474, only a very select band of pilots are let loose on the aircraft!

The BBMF's current 'Bomber Leader' (although he is due to leave at the end of the 1998 display season) is Sqn Ldr Dave Buchanan, who also acts as the Flight's Training Captain and is responsible for the conversion of new pilots onto the 'Lanc'. He joined the RAF in 1965 and spent several years flying the Avro Shackleton, so he is well versed in multi piston-engined tailwheel configured aircraft!

Chief Pilot on the CWH Lancaster is Don Fisher, a former Air Canada Captain with many hundreds of hours of piston-engined airliner flying 'under his belt'. Training Captain for 'KB726' is Don Schofield, a current Boeing 747 Captain with Air Canada. Don Schofield has been involved with the Canadian 'Lanc' for many years, and was one of the volunteer team who helped to restore the aircraft to flying condition.

"When our Lancaster's restoration was complete, Sqn Ldr Tony Banfield, who had just left BBMF in England, came across and test flew the bomber for us", remembers Don. "Because none of us at the museum at that time had any depth of experience with four-engined

Below: With 3,000 rpm and plus-7 boost on the engines, the pilots call for "brakes on, off, undercarriage up" and the 'Lanc' climbs away after take-off. (FP - Duncan Cubitt)

Bottom: Sometimes the Canadian Warplane Heritage Museum's Lancaster B.X 'KB726' operates off grass, but the crew members usually favour hard runways. (FP - Duncan Cubitt)

Airborne in 'KB726' — Al Topham monitors the engine and fuel instruments, while Don Fisher (Captain) and Dick Pulley (Co-pilot) fly the bomber. (FP - Robert Rudhall)

The crew of 'KB726' substitute a topside pass in place of an undercarriage down flyby during their display routine. (FP - Duncan Cubitt)

tailwheel aircraft we discussed operating and display procedures with Tony at great length. As a result of this our airshow routine is not unlike that flown by the BBMF's aircraft. However, we start our aircraft with a 4, 3, 2, 1, sequence on the engines, which is different to the RAF's Lancaster. We do this because the generators and compressors are configured differently on Canadian-built 'Lancs'.

"We also have a groundcrew member outside the aircraft who is 'plugged in' to the Lancaster's intercom system, that way he can talk to us and we can talk to him, keeping us in touch with what is happening outside the bomber during the start-up procedure. Being a civilian aircraft we tend to operate an airline-style series of checklists and drills, using a challenge and response routine. We always stick rigidly to these checks as none of us are flying the aircraft frequently enough to remember every single item."

Checklists and drills are an equally integral part of operating the BBMF's PA474. The current set of 'Flight Reference Cards' (detailing every check needed to fly the aircraft successfully) has been arrived at after many years of flying PA474 — its instructions are followed 'to the letter'.

The start-up routines are very similar for both aircraft — with the exception of the engine start sequence, as we've already explained. Once the engines have been started and the crew members are happy with the temperatures and pressures, etc, the controls will be set to idle (1,000rpm) and the bomber trundles forward

towards the active runway. In all there are 18 different pre-take off checks that have to be accomplished before the aircraft is ready to roll. This should explain why the 'Lanc' will sit at the end of the runway for a while before actually embarking upon its take-off run! In the cockpit, it's all go: trimmers - set for take-off; ignition switches - on, gyros uncaged; engine temperatures and pressures - within limits; fuel - master cocks on, flaps - 10° down indicating, selector to neutral; radiator shutters - automatic; superchargers - M gear; harnesses - tight and locked, and so it goes on before the

"We have timed take-offs in order to minimise airborne time in the Lancaster,"

co-pilot calls "pre-take off checks complete".

"We have timed take-offs in order to minimise airborne time in the Lancaster," explains Dave Buchanan. "The Navigator will have worked out a flight duration in order to get to our display location on time, and if we are departing our base at Coningsby we always check with the display organiser (by telephone) during the morning of the display to make sure of our slot time at the show. We always aim to arrive at the display venue, be it for a simple flypast at a village fete, or a major international airshow, more or less to the minute. Therefore working out our flying speed needed to arrive at the venue on time gives us the timed take-off.

"The normal sequence, if we are operating with a pair of fighters, is that the Spitfire will start his take-off first, followed by the Hurricane. Once I can see that the Hurricane is retracting its wheels, and there's no chance it aborting its take-off, I'll call for 3,000 revolutions per minute [rpm] on the engines with plus-7 boost setting. A final check over the instruments and we're off. After a short run, I'll lift the tail to get some directional stability, and the aircraft will normally lift off at around 90knots. She'll actually get airborne before that but we hold her on the ground until 90kts. Keeping the aircraft down, I'll get to 110kts as soon as I can before starting any significant climb out — 110kts is our minimum control speed if we should lose an engine during take-off."

The CWH has a slightly different approach to its take-offs, explains Don Schofield: "Because we have a slightly greater all-up weight than the RAF's aircraft, we take off with 3,000rpm and between plus-9 and plus-11 boost on the engines, depending on the runway length at the airfield we are using."

Back with the BBMF: "After take-off the two fighters join up in a loose formation and we fly down to the display location at around 3,000ft, depending on the height of the clouds," says Dave Buchanan. (The BBMF is not allowed to fly through cloud with any of the fighters or the Lancaster.)

"With 2,000rpm on the engines and boost as required we usually transit along at 150kts. Arriving at the display site we commence our first run past the crowd as a three-ship formation at between 150 and 170kts, and at 300ft. As we reach the end of the crowdline I'll call 'Memorial Flight, Break, Break, Go!' — the two fighters will then peel off, with the Spitfire displaying first. The Hurricane climbs to the rear of the airfield or display location and enters a holding pattern at 1,500ft. We in the Lancaster gently climb away and hold behind the crowd at 1,000ft. All the time we are holding we watch the Spitfires and then the Hurricane's display. The Hurricane will give a radio call one minute before the end of his routine, and that's my cue to get the Lancaster into a position where I can start my first flypast.

"Normally as the Hurricane is carrying out its victory roll [the final manoeuvre in its sequence] I'll be bringing the Lancaster through for its first run past the crowd at 100ft — 2,000rpm and plus-4 boost gives a speed of 180kts. The navigator starts the stopwatch as we pass the display datum point, after which we count up to nine or ten seconds depending on the length of the crowdline. Then it's engines at 2,400rpm and plus-4 boost and pull the bomber up and away from the crowdline, bringing the speed down to 150kts. Boost then comes down from plus-4 to minus-4, and the 'nav' opens the bomb bay doors. Flying back

"As the speed comes down to 130kts I'll call for plus-2 boost as we climb up to 400ft during the far part of the turn, ..."

towards the display datum I pull the aircraft round at 300ft to give the crowd a view of the underside of the Lancaster with the bomb doors open. As the speed comes down to 130kts I'll call for plus-2 boost as we climb up to 400ft during the far part of the turn, then the bomb bay doors are closed and we carry on with the turn clean."

During the Lancaster's display the co-pilot handles all the power changes, while the captain concentrates on flying the aircraft.

"Flying away from the crowd at around 30° I'll call for zero boost and 20° of flap," says Dave. "As we get the speed below 150kts we put the undercarriage down, and put the engines up to 2,850rpm. Making the turn back towards the crowd at 400ft, the 'nav' gives the two fighters a 'one minute rejoin' call. The gear-down pass in the 'Lanc' is flown at 110kts at 100ft. As we pass datum, I put the brakes on, then off, to stop the wheels spinning in the wind and call for plus-7 boost as I roll the bomber away from the display line. Leaving the power where it is, at 120kts we retract the flaps and the aircraft accelerates to 140kts.

"While we are doing this, the two fighters have caught us up and are rejoining in formation. The Hurricane always joins on the inside of the turn, due to its lower stalling speed. When the two fighter pilots are happy with their positions either side of the Lancaster they'll give us a call and we start to bring the three

"The 'nav' opens the bomb bay doors and we bring the aircraft round at 300ft to give the audience a good view of the 'Lanc's' underside." (FP - Duncan Cubitt)

Retracting the undercarriage PA474 banks away from the crowd. The pilot calls for "2,850rpm and plus 7 please" and the two fighters start to rejoin the Lancaster in formation for the final flypast. (FP - Robert Rudhall)

On normal transit flights the CWH's Lancaster cruises at 180kts, with 2,200rpm and plus 2 boost set up on the four Merlin engines. (FP - Robert Rudhall)

Landing a Lancaster can be a bit tricky at times, especially when there is a crosswind to contend with. BBMF's Bomber Leader, Sqn Ldr Dave Buchanan prefers to 'wheel' the aircraft with 'power on' onto the runway, raise the flaps to get better directional stability, chop the power on the engines and then let the tail fall slowly to the ground. (FP - Robert Rudhall)

aircraft back round for the final pass. Going around the turn at 140kts, with 2,000rpm and plus-2 boost, the formation flies past at 300ft, to exit the arena in the same direction as we arrived. Depending on the wind strength the 'Lanc's' display takes us about 5½ minutes to complete."

The CWH's Lancaster display is very similar to that flown by the BBMF, with the exception of the undercarriage-down pass. Instead, the pilots substitute a topside flyby, in which the bomber dumbbells out to one end of the crowdline and comes back in an arcing turn to show off the aircraft's upper surface. Engine rpms, boost settings and speeds are almost identical to that used on PA474 — probably as a result of the lengthy conversations with Tony Banfield after the restored aircraft's initial flight!

Landing the Lancaster has been the subject of much debate over the years. Wartime pilots have questioned why the aircraft is not 'three pointed' as was the 'norm' on the airfields of yesteryear, while current pilots favour the 'wheel it on' approach. Some pilots have, in the past, experienced difficulties during PA474's landing phase, so Dave Buchanan has devised a procedure whereby the aircraft is much more controllable when being brought in to land.

"We fly the downwind leg at zero boost and 2,400rpm, which gives us around 140kts. After lowering the undercarriage and flaps, by the end of the downwind leg we'll be at 115kts. Turning onto finals I'll call for 40° of flap, rpm up to 2,850 and boost remains at zero. Flaps then come down to 60°, reduce power in increments of 2lbs of boost, which gives us an 'over the fence' speed of 90kts. These days we keep the power on and wheel the bomber onto the runway. Once the

aircraft is down we 'slow cut' the engines and retract the flaps. By bringing the flaps up it does two things. It gives you more 'blow' over the aircraft's rudders for better directional control and it also keeps the bomber on the ground, preventing it from being skittish during the landing roll!"

This 'wheel it on' approach is also operated by the CWH crews, who like their BBMF counterparts, use a Dakota to train new pilots in the art of handling multi-engine tailwheel aircraft. "All of us who fly the Lancaster have a great passion for the aircraft", says Don Schofield, "and therefore we adopt a 'safety

"We fly the aircraft very conservatively, there is no latitude with the Lancaster"

first' attitude at all times, hence the use of the 'Dak' to make sure the pilots are 'at home' with that sort of aircraft. We fly the aircraft very conservatively, there is no latitude with the Lancaster to be the slightest bit aggressive. You have to anticipate what the aircraft is going to do in certain aspects of its operation. It's an aircraft with a great deal of inertia so you have to be on the ball at all times when you are airborne."

Both of the 'Lancs' are operated with strict crosswind limitations. Captains on the BBMF's PA474 are limited to a crosswind of 10kts, until the pilot has flown 50 hours on type, then the limit is raised to its permitted maximum of 15kts. This is the same for the Canadian aircraft.

While externally the bombers look much the same, the interiors are quite different. PA474's is in almost 100% wartime

configuration, with a good deal of its internal equipment intact. 'KB726', however, is virtually empty inside, so much so that as Don Schofield remarks "After stripping out a mass of equipment during the restoration process we had to put about 800lbs of ballast in the aircraft's tail in order to keep the centre of gravity where it should be." This, in simple terms, means that it is relatively easy to move around inside 'KB726', whereas you are in constant danger of banging your head in the British version.

PA474 is flown with a normal all-up weight of 45,000lb (20,400kg), with 'KB726's' max AUW is set at 53,000lb (24,000kg). The 'g' loading on the two aircraft is identical, with a maximum of 1.5g and a 'never exceed' of 1.8g, thus conserving the airframe's fatigue life as much as is possible.

The British and Canadian pilots are only too aware that the aircraft they are in charge of represent far more than countless pounds and dollars — they are living history, tributes to the many men who fought for, and lost their lives for, their countries. It is a remarkable testament to all those involved with PA474 and 'KB726' that as the new millennium approaches the world can still see one of the world's most effective bombing machines performing in its natural element. The sight of a Lancaster in flight can still raise a lump in the throat and bring a tear to the eye — and long may these two airworthy survivors continue to do so!

The author would like to express his thanks to the RAF Battle of Britain Memorial Flight and the Canadian Warplane Heritage Museum for their help in compiling this article.

My Private War with
Hitler's Gremlins

Just back from Berlin March 1/2, 1943, in Lancaster ED331: in doorway - W/O Sanderson (pilot), Sgt Tennant (flight engineer), Sgt Wigley (bomb aimer); standing - Sgt Campbell (rear gunner), Sgt Walshaw (wireless op), Sgt Kilby (navigator) and Sgt Mount (mid upper gunner).

Frank Walshaw's attempts to become operational on an RAF Lancaster squadron were, at first, frustrated by a run of gremlin trouble.

I WAS SMITTEN BY the flying bug in the late 1920s when I read of the exploits of Kingsford Smith, Amy Johnson, Amelia Earhart and Lindbergh. Whilst I was at grammar school, a Westland Wapiti force landed on the school sports fields. It was the first aeroplane I had seen on the ground and I was able to get close to it and, eventually, watch it take off. I devoured any reading matter on the subject of flying that I could find. At 17, I was employed as a sorting clerk and telegraphist at the Head Post Office in Barnsley, South Yorks. RAF Finningley was about 16 miles (25km) away and a friend and I used to cycle there to watch the Hampden bombers taking off and landing. I longed to fly in a Hampden and I was envious of an old school chum who had chosen the RAF as a career and was already

flying in Hampdens from Hemswell. Sadly he was killed in a crash near Caistor, Lincs, early in the war.

I passed my driving test soon after my seventeenth birthday, so a friend and I took our annual leave on a touring holiday of southern England in a 'clapped out' Singer Nine of 1931 vintage and which had cost £11. We returned north via Hendon where we halted to watch the aircraft activities. Throwing caution to the wind, we spent five shillings each on a short flight in a Percival Mew Gull — the first time either of us had flown. We eventually arrived home, broke, but very happy that we had been able to get airborne.

I persuaded one of my colleagues to join me in requesting permission from the Head Postmaster to enlist in the RAF. Permission

was granted and we went to the Sheffield recruiting office where, after a quick medical, we were enlisted as trainee aircrew. Being telegraphists we were to be Wireless Operators... "take it or leave it". My widowed mother was away on holiday and by the time she had returned home I had taken the King's Shilling at Padgate. I wasn't to see her again until our first 48-hour pass some months later. The colleague who enlisted with me was killed early in his tour of operations and his mother never forgave me for persuading him to enlist with me.

After Wireless and Air Gunnery Schools I was posted to 14 Operational Training Unit, Cottesmore. There I was involved in my first crash. At about 14.00 hours on December 23, 1941, I was in the crew of one of five Hampdens which took off on a cross-country training flight. It started to snow almost as soon as we were airborne and blizzard conditions quickly prevailed. We became lost and 41/2 hours after take-off we crashed on the banks of the River Colne estuary at Wivenhoe, Essex. By this time the snow was thick on the ground and helped cushion our impact, so the aircraft stayed in one piece. Luckily none of us was seriously injured and we were taken to a military hospital in Colchester. I had superficial head injuries, was badly bruised and had two broken fingers on my left hand. We were detained in hospital over Christmas and before returning to Cottesmore by train we went back to the site of the crash. Across the field where we had come down were rows and rows of power lines all converging on a power station nearby. In the darkness and in the blizzard conditions we had flown under them. Lucky us! When we got back to Cottesmore I learned that one of my friends on the same course had been killed in another Hampden crash on the same afternoon, they too had been forced down by the blizzard. I was then posted to 44 (Rhodesia) Squadron, Waddington on May 8, 1942, and was crewed with a pilot called Tompkins who was about to start his second tour of operations. We were doing

No 12 Course at No 1 Air Gunnery School, Pembrey 1941; author is in the middle row on the right.

No 44 Squadron was the first operational Lancaster unit, the first sorties being minelaying. (FP Collection)

all the usual conversion flight exercises and on the night of June 5/6 we were detailed to take eight bomb-aimers on a bombing exercise at Bassingham Fen, near Waddington, in Lancaster R5515. At about 3.30am on June 6, the bomb-aimers had finished their detail and we returned to Waddington. Having sent my landing signal I went to the rear of the plane, as it was very over-crowded up front, and I sat on the metal housing of the tail wheel assembly. When Tompkins attempted to land he got it all wrong and decided to overshoot but he'd left it too late and we crashed into a concrete gun emplacement on the eastern edge of the airfield. The tailwheel oleo leg came through its mounting hit me in the buttocks and catapulted me up into the roof of the aircraft. The Elsan toilet situated in front of the tailwheel mounting burst open and when I returned to a state of near consciousness I found myself lying in the Elsan's contents.

If you have never been hit in the rear by a swiftly accelerating hydraulic ram be assured by me that "it don't arf make yer eyes water". The 'blood-tub' soon arrived and they were pleased to find live customers to attend to — that was until they got a whiff of what I was lying in. I was taken to sick quarters and there the medics were not at all pleased by the all-pervading pong. I had lower spine and neck pain and it was decided to transfer me to Rauceby Hospital, Sleaford.

On returning to the Squadron I was still in some discomfort but was declared fit for flying duties. I joined a crew piloted by Ron Easom and as he was just converting to four-engined aircraft I went through the whole conversion programme again. On August 16, 1942, we took off on a daylight cross-country flight. In the bomb-aimer's position was a New Zealander called Dave Pullinger. Ron Easom was the pilot and

the flight engineer was Jack Fletcher. This was his familiarisation flight in a Lancaster. I was the wireless operator and in the mid-upper turret was a ground wireless operator who was with us just for the ride. Len Berrigan, a Canadian gunner, occupied the rear turret.

After a four-hour flight we were preparing to land when, as we began our approach to the airfield, we had an engine fire in the starboard inner. Easom told Fletcher to press the fire extinguisher button and to feather the propeller but in a panic he feathered the starboard outer prop. By this time we were in the funnel and with undercarriage down and some flap already applied we stalled and went into a yaw. I was looking out of the window and saw a church spire alongside us. I was sure that this was curtains for us all and yet it seemed an age before the final impact. We crashed on a pig farm in the village of Branston, about 2 miles (3.2km) to the east of Waddington. The aircraft broke in two, just aft of the main spar, and was instantly engulfed in flames. I had braced myself for the impact but the wireless transmitter broke from its mounting and hit me in the chest and upper abdomen — I sustained another neck injury. I remember being dragged from the plane by someone, at the time I didn't know who, and being carried away from the wreckage, to be laid on the grass by some nearby cottages. The pain in my chest was intense and I was coughing blood. The rescuers were able to save all except Pullinger in the nose of the plane and Fletcher who had been catapulted against the instrument panel

The 'gremlins' struck such that Frank Walshaw had to complete the Conversion Flight course three times whilst waiting to go operational with 44 Squadron — within nine months he had been involved in three crashes. (Andy Thomas Collection)

and then down into the nose. I was consciously aware of the two men who pulled the others free but could only look on helplessly. The fuel tanks had ruptured and blazing petrol was all around the wreckage. Some pigs were trapped under the wings, they were being roasted alive and their squeals were horrifying to hear. Ammunition was exploding all around when, from one of the cottages, emerged a little old lady bearing a tray full of refreshments. Her words, on nearing me, were "You'll be ready for a cup of tea luv". Nothing that was happening in the inferno around us seemed to faze her and she continued to dispense tea to we who had been rescued. In those days priority first aid treatment was a cup of sweet tea and a Woodbine.

The two men who had rescued us were a local farmer called Dick Taylor and a local butcher called Fred Kirk. With complete disregard for their own safety they had struggled to free us from a plane that was likely to have exploded at any moment. The 'blood-tub' was promptly on the scene and we were soon in the sick bay at Waddington. Ron Easom had been saved by his Sutton harness, the navigator escaped with severe bruising and Tommy Black in the mid-upper turret had hit his head on the rotating service joint and had sustained damage to one of his ears. Len Berrigan in the rear turret had hit his face on the graticule sight and had two black eyes and a broken nose. Dave Pullinger was killed outright and Jack Fletcher died in Bracebridge Heath Hospital that night.

Because I was still coughing blood I was admitted to Rauceby Hospital yet again. After examination and X-ray I was told that I had a fracture of the breast bone, fractured ribs and a whiplash neck injury. This time

my chest was tightly bound with sticking plaster and again I was fitted with the inevitable cervical collar. I was under the supervision of the ward orderly who had cared for me only a few weeks previously.

After about two weeks in hospital I was sent back to Waddington and told to have the plaster removed when the Squadron MO thought it appropriate, and I was granted a week's sick leave.

The aircraft in which we had crashed was Lancaster R5489. It had been named George and Lancaster R5548 had been named Elizabeth when King George VI and Queen Elizabeth had made an official visit to the factory at Yeadon on March 20, 1942.

By now I had begun to appreciate that flying was not as glamorous as I had fancifully believed. Within nine months I had been involved in three crashes, I had spent two

Aiming Point (AP) certificate awarded to the crew of Lancaster W4839 (KM-F) for the St Nazaire raid of February 28/March 1, 1943.

periods in hospital — what's more, I had been on the Squadron since May 8 and had not flown a single sortie against the Third Reich. I had come to the certain conclusion that Adolf had sent over his 'gremlins' to prevent me from ever overflying Germany. Truth to tell, I was terrified of ever stepping into another aircraft. I wasn't afraid of going on operations, as that was something that I had not yet experienced, but I dreaded being in another aeroplane crash. I suppose, in current jargon, I would have been diagnosed as suffering 'post traumatic stress syndrome'. Had I admitted it at that time it would have been labelled 'lack of moral fibre'. That was a stigma that I could not bear to carry.

On leave, I tearfully told my mother of my fears and of my struggle to overcome them. She took me in her arms and she said, "You joined the RAF whilst I was on holiday, you wanted to fly and you nearly broke my heart. If you pack in flying now you are not the son I know you to be. Go back, do your duty and God will see you through." I was thoroughly chastened by her words. She had been widowed twice, the first time she was newly married when she lost her husband in a coal mining accident, then my dad died at only 42 years of age. She was acquainted with grief and bore it stoically and with dignity.

On returning from leave my first priority was to find the two men who had rescued us from the crash. I cycled to Branston and called

Crews of 9 and 44 Squadrons the morning after the daylight raid on Milan (October 24, 1942).

at the local pub, The Plough (now demolished). The landlord knew where they both lived and I was able to find them and to convey to them our undying thanks. I spent several convivial evenings with them during the rest of my stay at Waddington.

Once again I was back in Conversion Flight awaiting, with trepidation, allocation to yet another new crew. I joined the crew of a young Australian pilot who was yet to convert to Lancasters so once again I had to

repeat all the conversion exercises. I had done so many take-offs and landings that I knew the Waddington circuit like the back of my hand. Until my fears gradually dissipated, at each take off and landing, I used to close my eyes and cling to the stanchion that ran from roof to floor beside the wireless operator's position. My new skipper's name was Colin Watt, the flight engineer was Jack Money, the navigator was John Charnock and the bomb-aimer was 'Tich' Hiscock. I was the wireless operator, the mid-upper gunner was Eddie Harrold and a Canadian called Tex Campbell was the rear gunner.

Frank Walshaw and Colin Watt with the appropriate backdrop of the BBMF Lancaster.

Colin was mature for his years and he inspired in me a confidence that had been lacking with my previous skippers and he helped me through the bad patches. He was like a father to the crew; he oozed confidence and he captained us with common sense and a caring discipline. We flew 20 operations together and the crew celebrated his 21st birthday on the way back from a raid on Kiel on the night of October 13/14, 1942. On a daylight sortie to Milan on October 24 we had

just crossed the French coast on our outward journey when we suffered a starboard engine malfunction due to a fractured drive-shaft. Colin flew to Milan, bombed the target and returned to base on three engines — more than 1,000 miles (1,600km). For this operation he was awarded an immediate DFM. On January 21, 1943, he was posted as an instructor to Wigsley. Soon afterwards he was repatriated to instruct Australian pilots on multi-engined aircraft. We were dismayed at losing our skipper and Colin was furious at having been taken off operations. The crew were dispersed. Jack Money became flight engineer to Wg Cdr Nettleton VC. They went missing on the night of July 12/13, 1943. John Charnock, the navigator, went to Transport Command. Eddie Harrold, the mid-upper gunner joined another crew and they failed to return from a raid on Cologne on February 2, 1943. I don't know what happened to Hiscock, the bomb-aimer.

Once again I was looking for a new skipper. Tex Campbell and I were lucky enough to join the crew of Warrant Officer 'Sandy' Sanderson. He had been an instructor on the Beam Approach Training Flight and had just returned to the Squadron to start his second tour of operations. With him I flew a further 16 operations and one with the Squadron Commander, Wg Cdr Ken Smales. In all, I completed 37 operations within the designated 200 hours. (Later on a tour was 30 operations.) When I left Waddington in March, 1943, I was the longest-serving wireless operator on the Squadron. Of 23 W/Ops who were posted with me to Waddington in May 1942 only I and a fellow W/Op called Jack Long were fortunate enough to survive to March, 1943. During that short period I shared a room with four different aircrew who all failed to return from operations. A mother's faith and God's will had brought me through a dark period in my life, assisted, not a little, by the skills of Colin Watt and 'Sandy 'Sanderson.

Lancaster survivors

PA474, the Battle of Britain Memorial Flight's (BBMF) Avro Lancaster B.I, cruises over the picturesque English countryside en-route to an airshow in July 1998. Currently painted as WS-J, 'The Bomber' represents W4964, a Lancaster of IX Squadron RAF, which took part in the attacks on the German battleship Tirpitz. (FP - Duncan Cubitt)

TB.I PA474, Battle of Britain Memorial Flight, RAF Coningsby, Lincs, UK

Of the 7,377 Lancasters built, only 16 examples currently exist in one piece, with just two of these remaining in airworthy condition. Robert Rudhall looks at the histories of most of these 'survivors'.

Without doubt one of the best-known 'warbirds' on the European airshow circuit, the BBMF's Lancaster PA474 has been flying as a preserved aircraft since November 7, 1967, and with its successful re-spar programme during the winter of 1995/96, the aircraft looks set to continue flying well into the next millennium! The Lanc's first major public appearance as a preserved machine was aptly at the Royal Review of the RAF which took place at RAF Abingdon in May 1968, and since then the bomber has averaged between 85 and 100 flying hours each year, appearing at events ranging from a village fete to major international air displays.

Built by Vickers Armstrong at Chester in 1945, PA474 was originally due to go to the Far East with the 'Tiger Force' as part of the offensive against the Japanese in the latter stages of World War Two. However, when the Americans dropped the Atomic bombs on Hiroshima and Nagasaki the war came to an abrupt end and PA474's secondment to the Far East was cancelled. Subsequently put into storage at 38 Maintenance Unit at RAF Llandow, the aircraft had just three hours

BBMF's Lanc pictured during its time with the Royal College of Aeronautics at Cranfield, when it was used as a test-bed for the various trials of aircraft wing sections. (Dave Allport Collection)

of flying time on the airframe!

After modifications at Coventry, PA474 was assigned to 82 Squadron at RAF Benson in November 1948 to be used as a photo reconnaissance aircraft. At that time, 82 Sqn was operating out of Takoradi in West Africa, and PA474 joined the unit on November 27, 1948. Spending the next few

years photographing much of the African continent '474 eventually returned to the UK and moved to Flight Refuelling Ltd (FRL) at Tarrant Rushton. The aircraft was loaned to FRL and was destined to be converted into a pilotless drone! However, before modification work commenced, the Air Ministry decided to use an Avro Lincoln

the stalwart hero

instead and PA474 was transferred to the Royal College of Aeronautics at Cranfield. Used for flight trials, the Lancaster was flown with different types of wing aerofoils fitted to the upper fuselage, including that of a Folland Midge and a Handley Page laminar flow wing.

In 1964 the Lancaster was replaced by a Lincoln and PA474 returned to RAF charge. It was then adopted by the Air Historical Branch, flown to 15 Maintenance Unit at Wroughton Airfield and was put into wartime markings, ready for inclusion in the then yet-to-be-built Royal Air Force Museum at Hendon.

Moved to RAF Henlow, the Lancaster was stored in the open, along with an Avro Lincoln, as the hangars were not big enough to accommodate the large four-engined bombers! As the new RAF Museum was still several years away, the then Commanding Officer of 44 Squadron at RAF Waddington (the first RAF unit to receive Lancs back in December 1941), Wing Commander D'Arcy managed to persuade the authorities at the Air Historical Branch to release PA474 into his care, so that at least the bomber could be housed inside!

With permission granted for a one-off ferry flight from Henlow to Waddington, PA474 lifted off on August 18, 1965, for her new home in Lincolnshire (Bomber County). Arriving at Waddington, the aircraft was thoroughly inspected and found to be in remarkable condition for its age. Subsequently '474 was worked on by a dedicated team of engineers and slowly but surely was put back into full flying trim, taking to the air again on November 7, 1967. After the initial test flight, approval was given for the aircraft to make 'occasional flights'. But once it could be seen that the Lancaster performed safely and that there was sufficient infrastructure to support it in an airworthy condition, permission was granted to fly the aircraft on a regular basis.

Operated on the UK airshow circuit by personnel from 44 Sqn at Waddington, the Lancaster was eventually transferred to the Battle of Britain Flight (BoBF) at RAF Coltishall, Norfolk, on November 20, 1973, thus keeping all of the RAF's historic piston-engined aircraft in one basket! Once

PA474 moved to Coltishall, the BoBF was re-named the Battle of Britain Memorial Flight (BBMF) in order to reflect the Flight's wider 'memorial' role.

When BBMF moved from Coltishall to Coningsby (its present home) in March 1976, the Lanc returned to 'Bomber County', much to the delight of the civilian Lincolnshire Lancaster Committee (now named Lincolnshire Lancaster Association), which had earlier been formed to bring the aircraft back to Lincolnshire. Some 18,000 signatures were collected on a petition, in just five weeks, to return the aircraft to Lincolnshire. Approaches were made to Members of Parliament and questions were even raised in the House of Commons as to the Lancaster's eventual resting place!

Over the years, PA474 has slowly been returned to its 'operational' wartime condition, inside and out. Gun turrets have been refitted, equipment has been sourced and

worldwide. Manned entirely by unpaid volunteers, Lincs Lancs works hard to support and present the BBMF in the best possible light.

PA474's markings are changed every time the bomber undergoes a major overhaul, i.e. every six years. It currently wears the markings W4964 of 9 Squadron, WS-J with the 'Johnnie Walker — Still Going Strong' legend on the nose. Due for a major overhaul in the winter of next year (1999) Lancaster PA474 will emerge in the next millennium wearing a fresh coat of paint and a different set of squadron codes.

Kept flying by a dedicated band of aircrew and groundcrew, PA474 is unique in that it is the UK's sole airworthy representative of the RAF's cadre of four-engined heavy wartime bombers, and as such serves as a living memorial to the 55,000-plus Allied airmen of Bomber Command who lost their lives fighting for the cause of freedom!

Captured in all of its glory, the Canadian Warplane Heritage Museum's Avro Lancaster B.X FM213 (C-GVRA) flies over the Ontario countryside. Wearing the colours of KB726, the 'Mynarski Memorial Lancaster' is the pride and joy of the CWHM's historic aircraft fleet. (FP - Duncan Cubitt)

returned to the aircraft's interior, much of this being accomplished with the enthusiastic support of the Lincolnshire Lancaster Association. The 'Lincs Lancs' — as it has become known — is now the official BBMF support group, with around 4,500 members

B.X 'KB726'/FM213, Canadian Warplane Heritage Museum, Hamilton, Ontario, Canada

SEPTEMBER 11, 1998, saw this Lancaster celebrate its tenth year of airworthiness with the Canadian Warplane Heritage (CWH) Museum in Canada. To restore and operate a Lancaster bomber for ten years is a remarkable achievement for a private organisation, and the CWH is currently the only civilian operators of an airworthy Lanc in the world!

Flown by a highly experienced crew, comprising serving and former airline pilots who have many hundreds (if not thousands) of hours flying multi piston-engined taildraggers in the past, the aircraft is the flagship of CWH and is the centre of attention whenever it flies.

Built in July 1945, it was one of the last batch off the assembly line at Victory Aircraft's factory at Malton, Ontario, before production stopped at FM229 in August 1945;

In a previous life FM213 served with 107 Rescue Unit at Torbay, Newfoundland, Canada, before being retired in 1964. Wearing a smart white and silver paint scheme, the Lancaster also carries copious amounts of 'DayGlo Red' on its wings and fuselage. (Larry Milberry)

however, FM213 was not officially accepted until late August due to a number of snags on the airframe.

The aircraft was put into storage at Trenton for five years and was eventually brought out for conversion into Lancaster 10MR/MP Maritime Reconnaissance/Maritime Patrol configuration by de Havilland at Downsview. Seeing service with 405 Squadron Royal Canadian Air Force (RCAF) at Greenwood, the aircraft suffered a very heavy landing and

'S for Sugar', R5868 in all her glory, stands at the entrance to the Bomber Command Hall at the Royal Air Museum, Hendon, London. (FP - Ken Delve)

groundloop at RCAF Trenton on January 15, 1952, which caused considerable damage to the undercarriage, airframe and engines. Repaired using a large proportion of Lancaster B.X KB895, FM213 re-entered operational service with 405 Sqn in the Search and Rescue role at RCAF Greenwood were it remained in an active condition up until its retirement from the military in November 1963.

Saved from the scrapman's axe by the Royal Canadian Legion branch at Goedrich, Ontario, it was purchased for preservation and static display for the princely sum of $1,200. Ferried to Sky Harbour Airport, the Lancaster was put on show while funds were raised to move it to a new home at Goedrich — where is was eventually positioned on three pylons in a flying attitude. Luckily (for the aircraft's subsequent history) it was mounted without any structural alterations being made to the airframe!

After a number of years on display in the open air the Lancaster was in dire need of a re-paint and it proved difficult to raise the necessary finance. After much deliberation, the aircraft was sold to the Canadian Warplane Heritage at Hamilton with a view to restoring it to airworthy condition. Airlifted beneath a 450 Squadron RCAF CH-47 Chinook, the Lancaster arrived at Hamilton International Airport on November 5, 1979. Although minor restorative work was carried out more or less straight away, the major rebuild programme did not start until early 1983, when a grant from the government, plus the employment of a chief engineer to oversee the project, gave the whole scheme a massive 'kick start'.

The amount of work needed to restore the bomber to flying condition is far too complex

to be included in this short précis of FM213's history (by far the best account is Bette Page's book 'Mynarski's Lanc'/Boston Mills Press), needless to say many thousands of man hours and many thousands of dollars would be expended before the four-engined bomber would fly again.

The bomber was taken aloft on its first post-restoration flight on September 11, 1988, by Tony Banfield, former Officer Commanding of the RAF's Battle of Britain Memorial Flight. FM213 was resplendent in its new colours representing KB726, the aircraft in which Flight Sergeant Andrew Mynarski gained his Victoria Cross on the night of June 12/13, 1944.

Since then the 'Mynarski Memorial Lancaster' has made many appearances all over Canada and North America and is looked upon with great affection by the many Canadian World War Two veterans who visit the CWH museum to pay homage to the famous Avro design.

B.I R5868, Royal Air Force Museum, Hendon, UK

The oldest surviving Lancaster in the world, the RAF Museum's R5868 has an enviable war record, having flown 137 operational sorties, including eight trips to Berlin and 16 to Germany's Ruhr! The aircraft actually started life on the Metropolitan Vickers production line in Manchester as an Avro Manchester (part of a batch ordered in 1939), but was completed as a Lancaster. It was transported to Woodford and assembled by Avro before being delivered to 83 Squadron at RAF Scampton on June 29, 1942. On the night of July 8/9, R5868 embarked on its first operational sortie when it 'visited' Wilhemshaven with a delivery of incendiary bombs. Two days later the Lancaster was airborne again, this time in daylight, for an attack on submarine yards at Danzig, where it dropped five 1,000lb (454kg) bombs, on what was then the longest bombing raid ever mounted by the RAF — a 1,500-mile (2,400km) round flight.

In late July, the was aircraft damaged when it was hit by fire from enemy flakships,

after bombing Hamburg. In mid-August, 83 Sqn moved to RAF Wyton, taking '5868 with it. This move saw the unit joining the RAF's Pathfinder Force, and on August 18/19 R5868 took part in the very first Pathfinder operation when it undertook target marking during a raid on Flensburg, close to the Danish/German border.

While serving with 83 Sqn the aircraft wore the code letters OL-Q, a change to these letters occurred when R5868 left 82 Sqn and joined 467 Sqn (Royal Australian Air Force) in August 1943. Moving from Wyton to Bottesford, the bomber was re-coded PO-S to replace 'S for Sugar'. While with 467 Sqn, R5868 took part in the Battle of Berlin, visiting the 'Big City' eight times — and it didn't always get away scot-free. On one occasion, on November 26/27, 1943, the Lancaster was coned in searchlights after completing the bombing run. Enemy fighters were attacking the bomber stream heavily and '5868 is reported to have collided with another Lancaster — great skill was needed to keep the bomber on an even keel. It took four hours to fly back to England, and the right rudder had to be applied for the entire flight back!

On a diversion landing at Linton-on-Ouse (due to a low fuel load), the aircraft landed fast — heavy braking then caused it to groundloop at the end of the runway. On external inspection it was found that the Lancaster had lost a 5ft (1.5m) section off its port wing! The aircraft was returned to the manufacturers for major repairs and did not return to operational flying until February, 1944.

R5868's final operational flight took place on April 23, 1945, when it returned to Flensburg to attack German U-boats. The aircraft was unable to deliver its bomb load as the target was covered in cloud. The Lancaster had flown over 500 hours on 'ops' and dropped around 500 tons of bombs. Only one other Lancaster (ED888 from 103 & 576 Sqns) flew more operational flights. Both of these war-weary aircraft survived the war, but R5868 is the only one still extant — ED888 was scrapped in 1947.

Postwar, R5868 was declared a 'non effective airframe' and was put into storage, along with many other Lancs at Wroughton. In 1956 the bomber was transferred to the RAF's Historical Aircraft Collection and in 1959 it was moved by road to RAF Scampton to take up gate guardian duties. Originally R5868 was to have remained 'on guard' at Scampton, while PA474 would be inserted into the RAF Museum at Hendon. However, after '474 was returned to airworthy condition it was decided to put R5868 into the Hendon complex.

From the initial survey to ascertain how much work was required, it was found that the Lancaster had weathered the years outside well, and was duly dismantled and moved to Hendon by road. Restored by a team of engineers from RAF St Athan, the Lancaster emerged in her 467 Sqn markings, and was positioned in pride of place when the RAF Museum eventually opened on November 29, 1972.

After spending 11 years parked in the far corner of the museum, the Lancaster was on the move again, but this time only a few yards! The newly-built RAF Bomber Command Hall was unveiled in 1983, and the Lancaster now occupies prime position at its entrance. Displayed in a flying attitude, with a sky backdrop and the sound of Lancasters taking off, R5868 is without doubt one of the most historic aircraft on show anywhere in the UK. Many visitors to the museum gaze in awe at the impressive bomb tally on its nose, finding it hard to believe that the four-engined bomber somehow managed to survive against all the odds pitted against it. 'S for Sugar' remains at Hendon as a fine memorial to RAF Bomber Command and the men who went to war in the Lanc.

B.I W4783, Australian War Memorial, Canberra, Australia

Currently being prepared for dismantling and removal from the Australian War Memorial (AWM) museum at Canberra, Lancaster I W4783 'G for George' is to undergo an extensive restoration, after spending many years inside the museum building.

Operated by the Royal Australian Air Force's 460 Squadron in the UK during World War Two, this particular aircraft was flown by 29 different crews and completed some 90 operational sorties over enemy-occupied territory. The Lancaster sustained damage from enemy flak and night fighters on 20 separate occasions!

In 1944 it was flown to Australia in order to stimulate interest and support in the war effort 'back home'. While in Australia, the

Lancaster was issued with the Australian military serial A66-2 and flown around to entice people to buy War Bonds. Those who pledged A£100 were rewarded with a 20-minute flight, while those who gave A£10 were allowed inside the aircraft on the ground. W4783/A66-2 was finally retired from military service in 1950 and presented to the Australian War Museum for preservation and display. The aircraft has remained with the AWM ever since. **Craig P Justo**

B.VII NX611, Lincolnshire Aviation Heritage Centre, UK

Built by Austin Motors at Longbridge, near Birmingham, NX611 was rolled out of the factory as a Lancaster B.VII in April 1945, but was just too late to take part in World War Two in Europe. The first of 150 production Lanc B.VIIs, it was finished to Far East configuration and fitted with a

East Kirkby's NX611 'Just Jane' runs up her four Merlin engines as the BBMF's PA474 (in the background) positions for a flypast 'over the top'. (FP - Robert Rudhall)

Martin mid upper gun turret instead of the usual Fraser Nash variant.

After the Americans brought the war to an abrupt end, NX611 was declared surplus to requirements and put into storage at 38 Maintenance Unit, Llandow. Later sold to the French Aéronavale for a reported sum of £50,000, the Lancaster was given the new identity of WU15 and repainted in midnight blue colours. Collected from Woodford by a French ferry crew on May 30, 1952, the aircraft then spent the next ten years based at Brittany, Port Lyautey and Agadir, and was used for maritime patrols and air sea rescue duties. In 1962 the aircraft was overhauled, repainted overall white and flown to Noumea, New Caledonia, 1,000 miles (1,600km) east of Australia. The Lancaster then undertook patrol, ASR, liaison and general communication duties over a wide area of the Pacific Ocean until being withdrawn from service in 1964.

It was around this time that the Historic Aircraft Preservation Society (HAPS) in the UK started to look at the feasibility of preserving a Lancaster bomber, as at that time there wasn't a single airworthy example in Britain. After some lengthy negotiations with the French authorities, the Lancaster was donated to HAPS, on the proviso that HAPS would fund the return flight to England! NX611 was flown to Bankstown in Australia in August 1964 ready for HAPS to collect it and fly it to the UK. It had been calculated that it would cost in the region of £10,000 to get the Lancaster back to England, and with many donations from private individuals and generous help from a number of commercial organisations, sufficient money was raised to overhaul the bomber and embark on the long trip home!

April 25, 1965, saw the Lancaster leave Mascot Airfield, near Sydney, on the first leg of its flight to the UK. The aircraft retained its white Aéronavale markings, but was allocated the British Civil registration G-ASXX. After an epic flight, taking 19 days and almost 70 hours flying time, the Lancaster touched down at Biggin Hill in Kent on May 13 to coincide with the opening of the annual Biggin Hill Air Fair. Then the world's sole flying Lancaster, NX611 (G-ASXX) proved to be the 'star of the show'.

After its debut at Biggin Hill, the aircraft

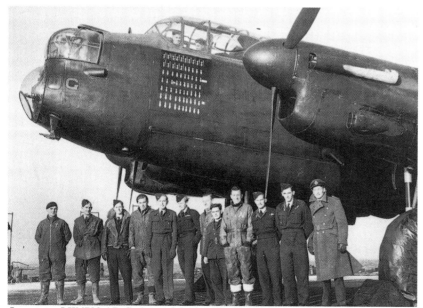

Lancaster I W4783 AR-G pictured during World War Two at RAF Binbrook, along with its air and ground crews, after it had completed 70 operational sorties. The aircraft went on to complete 90 'ops' and is currently preserved by the Australian War Memorial museum at Canberra. (via Harry Holmes)

underwent a two-year overhaul and repaint, before emerging in standard RAF Bomber Command markings, with the codes HA-P (standing for Historic Aircraft Preservation Society), co-incidentally the codes of 218 (Gold Coast Squadron which flew Lancs during World War Two. HAPS intended to operate the bomber on the European airshow circuit but due to prohibitive running costs (even in those days), the aircraft made few public appearances and only flew 14 times after returning to the UK. By 1968 the RAF's PA474 was airworthy and HAPS lacked sponsors and funding to keep NX611 in the air.

HAPS was subsequently wound up and the Lancaster's ownership was transferred to Reflectaire Ltd. Moved from Biggin Hill to Lavenham, the bomber eventually ended up based at Hullavington, before being finally flown to Blackpool on June 26,

out of the hangar and ran all four of its Rolls-Royce Merlin engines for the first time in many years!

The Lancaster, now named 'Just Jane' and 'City of Sheffield', carries out regular engine runs and taxi demonstrations at East Kirkby during the summer months. Lately it has been taking visitors to the museum back in time by performing night-time taxies, giving a taste of what it must have been like on a Bomber Command airfield during World War Two.

Continuing work has resulted in the bomb bay doors and flaps becoming operable again, and it is planned to get the nose and tail gun turrets working again in the future. Now very much a 'live' Lancaster, NX611 is surrounded at East Kirkby by a willing cadre of volunteers who are all proud to be associated with this charismatic bomber.

French Aéronavale (French Navy). Converted for maritime surveillance duties and carrying the serial WU16, it was flown to the South Pacific where it was operated from the French Protectorate of Tahiti (Papeete) and New Caledonia (Noumea). In 1962 the aircraft was replaced in service by the Lockheed P2V-7 Neptune, and the French Government presented the Lancaster to the Air Force Association (Western Australian Division). Flown to Perth, NX622 was repainted in an authentic RAF camouflage scheme and put on display to raise funds for the Royal Australian Air Force Association. Some 20 years later the bomber was put under cover at the AFA's Heritage Museum, located at Bull Creek on the outskirts of Perth, where it remains to this day. **Craig P Justo**

B.VII NX665, Museum of Transport, Technology and Social History, Auckland, New Zealand

Currently the only example of a Lancaster bomber on display in New Zealand, NX665 is another of the French Aéronavale aircraft and at the time of writing is displayed wearing two different identities — PB457/SR-V on the port side of the fuselage and ND752/AA-O on the starboard. Built by Austin Motors in June 1945, NX665 was too late to see service in World War Two and was put into storage at 38 Maintenance Unit, where it remained until 1951.

One of the Lancasters supplied to the French Aéronavale, NX665 took up the new identity of WU13 and in 1959 was assigned to a training unit at Agadir, Morocco, afterwards serving with Escadrille 55S at Agadir and Khourigba. June 1961 saw the Lancaster moving to Noumea, New Caledonia, with Escadrille 9S, where it carried out regular patrols, radar calibration, aerial photography and general 'flag waving' duties for the French.

With a shortage of spares, coupled with increasing maintenance costs, the Lancasters were retired — WU13 was flown to Whenuapai and presented to the people

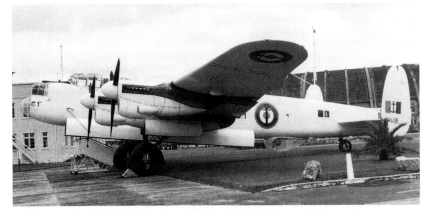

Avro Lancaster B.VII NX622 pictured here during its French Aéronavale service when its identity was WU16. (via Harry Holmes)

1970. Intended to be the centrepiece of a new aviation museum, NX611 enjoyed a bit of screen stardom when it was used in the making of the 1970s television series 'A Family at War'. When the museum venture eventually fell through, the Lancaster was put under the auctioneer's hammer on April 29, 1972. Acquired by Lord Lilford of Nateby, the bomber was dismantled and moved by road to RAF Scampton, where it took up gate guardian duties on a ten-year loan to the RAF agreement. At the end of the loan period, NX611 was purchased by Fred and Harold Panton, two farmers from East Kirkby. Plans were then set in motion for a new aviation museum to be based at East Kirkby, a former RAF Bomber Command airfield. The Lancaster remained at Scampton for five more years before being moved by road to a new hangar at East Kirkby. Forming the centrepiece of the Lincolnshire Aviation Heritage Museum, the bomber was renovated to improve its overall condition and in recent years has undergone an enormous amount of work to bring it up to taxiing standard. Two engineers, Ian Hickling and Roy Jarman, were engaged to bring the bomber back to life and their determined labours came to fruition in July 1995, when NX611 was proudly towed

B.VII NX622, Air Force Association, Bull Creek, Perth, Australia

One of the former Western Union machines, NX622 currently serves as a memorial to all the Australian bomber crews who fought in the European theatre of operations during World War Two. Originally built for the Royal Air Force as NX622, it was subsequently one of 54 Lancaster bombers acquired by France for service with the

Pictured during its French Aéronavale career, when it wore the serial WU13, Lancaster B.VII NX665 is currently preserved in the Museum of Transport, Technology and Social History at Auckland, New Zealand. (via Harry Holmes)

of New Zealand as a goodwill gesture. At the time of its last flight, NX665/WU13 had a grand total of 2,348 flying hours to its credit.

Having been dismantled and transported to Auckland, keen volunteers have since restored the aircraft into markings worn by a pair of Lancaster IIIs operated by 75 Sqn and 101 Sqn during World War Two. On the port side the Lancaster wears the codes SR-V with the serial PB457 of 101 Sqn based at Ludford Magna, and the starboard side, the fuselage is adorned with the codes AA-O and serial ND752, as worn by a Lanc of 75 (New Zealand) Sqn based at Spilsby.

B.X FM104, Canadian National Exhibition Grounds, Toronto, Canada

Looking a lot healthier than it has done for many years, Lancaster B.X FM159 is preserved by the Nanton Lancaster Society Museum in Alberta, Canada. (Nanton Lancaster Society)

After many years being displayed on a plinth close to the Toronto waterfront, it is hoped that this particular Lancaster will be brought down from its lofty perch and restored to museum static display in the near future. FM104 saw service with 428 Sqn (RCAF) in the UK before returning to Canada in June 1945. Modified to Lancaster 10MR configuration, the bomber flew with 10 Rescue Unit, based at Torbay, Newfoundland, until retirement in 1962. Put on the plinth in Toronto in 1965, the aircraft has suffered over the years from the elements and sporadic bouts of vandalism. (FP - Duncan Cubitt)

B.X FM136, Calgary Aerospace Museum, Alberta, Canada

While the exterior of this Lancaster looks a little on the rough side, the interior is absolutely immaculate — thanks to the efforts of the restoration team at the Calgary Aerospace Museum. FM136 was built by Victory Motors at Malton, Ontario, and sent to the UK in early 1945. Put straight into storage at 20 MU and then 32 MU, the aircraft flew back to Canada in August 1945. Converted to Maritime Patrol configuration the Lancaster then went into RCAF service with 407 Sqn, and was stationed at Comox, British Columbia, where it provided sterling service for the following 16 years until it was retired on April 10, 1961. One year later, the bomber was repainted to represent Lancaster I VN-N of 50 Sqn, RAF, and was moved to Calgary International Airport and positioned on top of a plinth. Sadly, as part of the procedure, the aircraft's main spar was cut through. Brought down from the plinth in April 1992, the aircraft was given another repaint,

B.X FM159, Nanton Lancaster Society Museum, Nanton, Alberta, Canada

Like many other Canadian-built Lancasters, FM159 was too late to see operational service in World War Two, instead spending most of its time in England in storage at maintenance units. Flown back to Canada for preparation for service against the Japanese, these plans were dropped after the atomic bombs were dropped on Hiroshima and Nagasaki. In the autumn of 1945, FM159 was flown to Fort Macleod, Alberta, and once again put into storage. It was one of many aircraft which stood in long rows at the former British Commonwealth Air Training Plan air base. However, because of its low airtime, FM159 was chosen to be reactivated as a maritime reconnaissance aircraft for the RCAF, and in June 1953 was flown out for conversion to Lancaster 10MR standards by de Havilland. Becoming operational at RCAF Greenwood, Nova Scotia, it served with 103 Rescue Unit,

Now safely down from its pole, Avro Lancaster B.X FM136 is receiving a lot of care and attention from the restoration team at the Calgary Aerospace Museum. (Ken Delve)

this time emerging as NA-P of 428 (RCAF) Squadron.

Until covered accommodation can be arranged for the Lancaster, restoration work has concentrated on its interior, which is now almost 100% complete, belying its well-used external appearance.

before being further modified by Fairey Aircraft and serving with 407 Sqn, based at Comox, British Columbia. During its sojourn with 407 Sqn, FM159 became a much-travelled aircraft, flying to places as far apart as England, Alaska and even Hawaii. Struck off charge in 1960, three aircraft enthusiasts purchased FM159 and towed it across grain fields to Nanton, where it was preserved as a tourist attraction.

Sadly, over the years, vandals broke many of the aircraft's Perspex panels and stole numerous instruments. Subsequently donated to the town of Nanton, the Lancaster was positioned behind a fence to keep the vandals at bay, but little else was done to preserve it.

In 1985 the Nanton Lancaster Society was formed specifically to look after the ageing bomber and positive steps were taken to improve the its condition. After a blizzard in 1989, which caused more damage to the Lancaster, the society members started a fund-raising appeal to construct a building so that it could be housed indoors. By 1991 a $500,000 building was completed and FM159 was wheeled inside. Since then considerable work has been carried out on the Lancaster and the aircraft is slowly but surely being restored back to its wartime configuration.

Red propeller spinners contrasting with the silver paint on the wings and fuselage, Lancaster B.X/10AR KB882 is preserved in static condition at St Jacques Airport, Edmunston, Canada. (Robert Rudhall Collection)

Although displayed minus any gun turrets, Lancaster B.X FM212 is kept in good condition and wears the codes EQ-W representing its operational time with 408 Sqn, RCAF. (Jim Buckel)

B.X FM212, City of Windsor, Ontario, Canada

Like many of the preserved Canadian-built Lancs FM212 spent many of its early years in storage, eventually being modified to 10MR standard. The aircraft later saw service with 408 Sqn, RCAF, before being retired from active use and put into storage again! Struck off air force charge in October 1964, the Lancaster was moved to Jackson Park Gardens in Windsor, Ontario, and mounted on a plinth for display purposes. Initially painted in an inaccurate colour scheme and coded CF-S, the bomber has in more recent times been given an authentic coat of Bomber Command camouflage colours and currently wears the 408 Sqn RCAF codes EQ-W.

B.X KB839, Canadian Forces Base Greenwood, Canada

Little is known of this particular Lancaster's history apart from that it was built by Victory Aircraft at Malton, Ontario, Canada, and served with 419 (Moose) Sqn, RCAF.

The unit's last operational sortie of World War Two was on April 25, 1945, and by June KB839 was back in Canada for conversion to 10AR configuration. After its military flying career came to an end, the Lancaster was moved to CFB Greenwood for display in 1965, where it resides to this day.

B.X KB882, St Jacques Airport, Edmunston, Canada

Entering service with 428 (Ghost) Sqn, RCAF, in March 1945, the unit left Bomber Command and flew back to Canada with its aircraft in June 1945, disbanding on September 5. Modified to 10AR standard, KB882 went on to serve with 408 Sqn as part of Air Transport Command and was based at Rockcliffe, Ottawa, during the early 1960s.

Struck off charge on May 26, 1964, the Lancaster, which by that time was fitted with a modified 'long nose', was flown to St Jacques Airport near Edmunston for preservation and static display. Still wearing its RCAF Air Transport Command colours and markings, KB882 is one of the few Lancasters preserved in this configuration.

B.X KB889, Imperial War Museum, Duxford Airfield, UK

The only example of a Canadian-built B.X in the UK, the Imperial War Museum's

Pictured in 1961 at RCAF Trenton during its service with 408 Sqn, Lancaster B.X KB839 is maintained in static condition at CFB Greenwood, Nova Scotia, Canada. (Larry Milberry)

Lancaster has had a chequered career. One of the 430 Lancs built by the Victory Aircraft Company at Malton, Ontario, Canada, it rolled off the production line in late 1944, and was flown across the Atlantic to Britain, where it joined 428 Squadron, (RCAF) in April 1945. From June, the bomber spent several months based at RAF St Mawgan in Cornwall before starting its journey back to Canada. On arrival in the 'land of its birth' KB889 was stored for a period before entering service with Maritime Air Command at Greenwood AFB. Later the aircraft was converted for maritime patrol duties, emerging in 10MP configuration, after which it was flown by 107 Rescue Unit, based at Torbay, Newfoundland. By 1962 it was back in storage once again, but served for one month only with Air Transport Command before being consigned to storage yet again.

In 1963, KB889 was sent to the breakers yard, but was returned because it was in too good a condition for scrapping! Sold in 1965 to Age of Flight Ltd at Niagara Falls, some three years later it was purchased by a private individual who started an ambitious restoration to flying condition. This rebuild is thought not to have been completed and by early 1984 KB889 was acquired by Doug Arnold's Warbirds of Great Britain Collection, shipped to the UK and registered as G-LANC. A rebuild, using parts of Avro Lincoln RF342 (G-APRJ) was contemplated, but not embarked upon. By 1986 the bomber, thanks to the help of the National Heritage Memorial Fund, had been purchased by the Imperial War Museum at Duxford, where a full static restoration was started. After much work the bomber was unveiled in its original 428 Squadron (RCAF) colours (coded NA-I) on November 1, 1994, and remains to this day one of the major aircraft attractions at Duxford.

B.X KB944, National Aviation Museum, Ottawa, Canada

Built by Victory Aircraft at Malton, KB944 was flown to the UK, arriving on March 8, 1945, and was allocated to 425 (Alouette) Sqn RCAF, based at Tholthorpe, Yorkshire, as part of 6 Group. By June, the bomber was on its way back to Canada and storage at Fort McLeod, Alberta. In 1952 it was being used by 404 Sqn and had been converted to Lancaster 10S standard, the conversion having been carried out by Fairey Aviation at Halifax, Nova Scotia.

On January 28, 1957, the Lancaster was transferred to a RCAF storage unit at Dunnville, Ontario, from whence it was allocated to the National Aviation Museum on May 11, 1964.

The Lancaster has remained in the care of the NAM ever since, and has been returned to 100% stock military configuration. It currently wears the markings, NA-P, representing an aircraft of 428 Squadron, RCAF.

Basking in the sunshine during a rare 'trip' out of the Duxford hangars in 1995, KB889 is a fine example of the aircraft restorers' skill. It is hoped that one day the Lancaster will be parked alongside the BBMF's PA474 during one of its frequent airshow visits to the IWM's airfield. (FP - Robert Rudhall)

Lancaster survivors			
Mark	Serial	Location Status	
B.I	R5868	RAF Museum, Hendon, UK	SD
B.I	W4783	Australian War Museum, Canberra, Australia	SD
B.I	W4964	Newark Air Museum, UK	F
B.I	DV372	Imperial War Museum, London, UK	N
B.I	PA474	RAF Battle of Britain Memorial Flight, Coningsby, UK	A
B.VII	NX611	Lincolnshire Aviation Heritage Centre, East Kirkby, UK	T
B.VII	NX622	Air Forces Association, Perth, Australia	SD
B.VII	NX664	Ailes Anciennes, Le Bourget, Paris, France	R
B.VII	NX665	Museum of Transport & Technology, Auckland, Australia	SD
B.X	FM104	National Exhibition Ground, Toronto, Canada	SD
B.X	FM136	Calgary Aerospace Museum, Alberta, Canada	R
B.X	FM159	Lancaster Society Museum, Nanton, Canada	R
B.X	FM212	City of Windsor, Ontario, Canada	SD
B.X	FM213	Canadian Warplane Heritage Museum, Hamilton, Canada	A
B.X	KB839	Canadian Forces Base Greenwood, Canada	SD
B.X	KB848	St Jacques Airport, Edmunston, Canada	SD
B.X	KB889	Imperial War Museum, Duxford, UK	SD
B.X	KB944	National Aviation Museum, Rockcliffe, Canada	SD
B.X	KB976	Weeks Air Museum, Florida, USA	S

Key: **A** = Airworthy, **F** = Fuselage section, **N** = Nose section, **R** = Under Restoration, **S** = Stored, **SD** = Static Display, **T** = Taxiable.

Lancaster B.X KB944 pictured in 1967 enjoying a rare airing from the National Aviation Museum at Ottawa, Canada. (Larry Milberry)

Green Endorsement

It was not only enemy action that caused problems for Bomber Command crews; Stephen Dyer relates how one Australian pilot earned a 'Green Endorsement'.

Another PO-U, this one being PB754, of 467 Squadron at Waddington in early 1945. (Andy Thomas Collection)

AWARDS TAKE MANY forms. Some reflect individual gallantry, others signify special achievements, whilst many honour commitment to a specific campaign. The 'Green Endorsement' appears only in an aircrew logbook and is awarded in recognition of 'professionalism'.

Walter (Kitch) Boxsell, an Australian pilot with 467 Squadron at Waddington, was awarded a 'Green Endorsement' following a mission on October 28/29, 1944.

"We flew out over the 'drome in the opposite direction to which we were going to set course. If you had ten minutes to waste you flew out for five minutes and back for five minutes. On this operation the maximum height we could fly at was 2,000ft. We were coming back towards the aerodrome to set course at about 1,500ft. Another Squadron aircraft had taken off late and he was climbing steeply and dodging another aircraft. He was in a vertical bank when he hit me. His wingtip went in and ripped a hole in the mainplane and bashed the bottom fin. I spun immediately, or started to spin, and that's when I asked the boys to put on parachutes. That was the drill anyway. Drill — you do it — it comes naturally. She started to go and the immediate reaction was 'Put on parachutes' — first thing I said. I told them to get out, knowing we had only 1,500ft under us.

"Three of them had gone by the time I started to take control again. From there we just climbed out to sea to jettison the bomb load. They had three emergency aerodromes in this part and Carnaby was the nearest one to us."

Emergency landing grounds (ELGs) had been established at Woodbridge and Manston in 1943, followed by Carnaby in March 1944; by the time Kitch needed their services they had handled nearly 5,000 emergency landings. One in five of those limping in had suffered battle damage, and half had suffered technical failures or a shortage of petrol. In October 1944 alone, the ELGs had taken more than 800 aircraft which might otherwise have crashed at their home bases, disrupting operational flying.

A secret report in Emergency Landing Service Bulletin No 10 takes up the story:

"At 2345 hours on the night of October 28/29 an aircraft gave a 'Mayday'. Carnaby

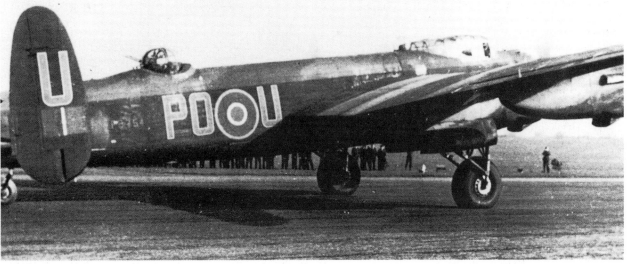

The 'Green Endorsement' added to Kitch Boxsell's logbook. (via the author)

> Soon after take off on an operational sortie F/o Boxsell's aircraft was involved in a mid air collision in bad weather. Despite severe damage F/o. Boxsell regained control, proceeded out to sea to jettison his bombs, and made a skilfull belly landing at an emergency airfield. His good captaincy saved his crew from injury.
>
> D. Bonham Carter
> Group Captain,
> Commanding, R.A.F. Station,
> WADDINGTON.
>
> 25 November 1944.

467 Squadron formed in November 1942 and flew Lancaster throughout the war; LM233 shown here also served with I5, 35 and 635 Squadrons. (Ken Delve Collection)

answered but received no reply. The aircraft was heard approaching at 0006 hours and the pilot called that he had a damaged port wing and was attempting an emergency landing. This message was repeated again at 0008 hours, but by this time the aircraft had proceeded out to sea and although Carnaby called several times on R/T, no reply was received. The aircraft R/T was not receiving."

At an operational base, Kitch's lack of radio control would have made it impossible for him to announce his arrival and to be placed in the landing queue. His undetected approach could have endangered other aircraft. Carnaby existed to prevent such problems. Its runway was 250 luxurious yards wide, divided into three parallel strips.

Kitch needed a lot of room, because, as the Bulletin recorded:

"In the collision the aircraft had its port aileron damaged and a large hole torn in the outer mainplane. The fin and rudder were also damaged and the pilot, engineer and navigator regained control of the aircraft [with] a rope from the [control] column to the window taking up the strain of the column, to assist keeping the aircraft on an even keel.

"All the lights at Carnaby had been exposed for some time and at 0030 hours the aircraft was heard approaching from the east. The aircraft touched down on the emergency runway 500 yards from the end, bounced and touched again on the overshoot."

Kitch and his crew supplied what Carnaby judged to be the outstanding incident of its 147 emergencies that month. The incident also demonstrated the effectiveness of aircrew training in emergency procedures. From the beginning of their flying careers the airmen had been drilled and drilled in handling the unpredictable in the most effective way. Parachute drill determined the order of jumping and Kitch's crew followed it. Aircrew were briefed to use the green-lit lane at Carnaby if they couldn't make radio contact. Despite the other demands on his attention at the time, this is precisely what Kitch did.

Just as operational flying had its drills and routines, so too did the RAF's system

of recognising and rewarding exemplary performance. At the informal level there was the 'Green Endorsement', awarded by a senior officer. It was a certificate on green paper (or in green ink) attached to the airman's logbook. Kitch's read:

"Soon after taking off on an operational sortie, F/O Boxsell's aircraft was involved in a mid-air collision in bad weather. Despite severe damage, F/O Boxsell regained control, proceeded out to sea to jettison his bombs, and made a skilful belly landing at an emergency airfield. His good captaincy saved his crew from injury."

The 'Green Endorsement' was a rare enough occurrence, and most unusual for a first operational sortie. Of more practical value to the crew was the order from No 5 Group RAF that the aborted sortie would count as one operation. In theory they had only another 29 to go to complete a tour and have a rest from operational flying. In theory... By early 1945 the shortages of crews

to prosecute the war over Europe had caused the tour of operations to be raised to 35 sorties. They had completed 32 when the number reverted to 30 — "So we went out to celebrate".

There is a footnote to this story which demonstrates that the past is a mysterious territory. Despite their aura of precision, official records are inconsistent. Kitch's logbook records that he was airborne for 140 minutes in PO-U LM636.

The 467 Squadron Diary identifies his Lancaster Mk III as LM746 and the flight time as 138 minutes, landing at 0032. The Carnaby report has him still airborne at 0033. He recalls three of the crew parachuting; the Diary claims four!

(The aircraft record cards show that LM746 was 'damaged beyond repair' in a collision with NN714. The latter aircraft was repaired but was lost on a mission to Harburg on November 12, 1944.)

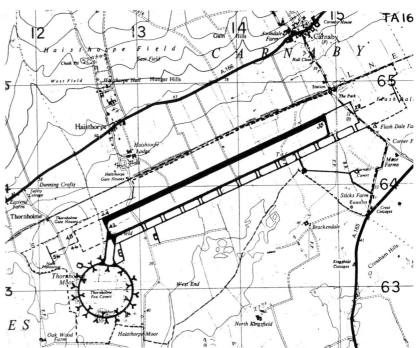

The emergency landing airfield at Carnaby saved a great many aircraft. (Ken Delve Collection)

When it comes to editorial quality, outstanding photography a

AIR Enthusiast

...a definitive read on a wide range of subjects

Within every page of *AIR Enthusiast* can be found deep, authoritative aviation history from the earliest days of flight up to the heady achievements of the 1960s. World-respected, *AIR Enthusiast's* style has always been to provide a comprehensive read on a wide range of subjects backed by a barrage of illustrative material, archive photographs, general arrangement drawings, airbrush detail views and, of course, cutaway diagrams and scale plans. Articles written by the very best of researchers mean that every issue is crammed with the definitive word on a broad spread of topics. *AIR Enthusiast* is an eighty-four page perfect bound magazine and its treatment of aviation history is quite unique. Each issue's coverage is truly international and always absorbing and will progress on to an avidly sought-after collector's item. Be you historian, modeller or keen to follow aviation history as deeply as possibly, *AIR Enthusiast* is the journal for you.

Bi-Monthly

AIR International

Comprehensive coverage of the latest civil and military aircraft...

AIR International was established in 1972 and ha a proven track record world-wide in authoritat reporting and coverage of the full spectrum of aviation subjects. Visits to world-wide airshows a major aviation industries by our editorial team keep our readers abreast of all the military, commercial and aerospace industry news. It's this resulting and comprehensive coverage that is the hallmark of *AIR International*. Written by some of the most respected and competent writers in the aerospace world, these technical assessments include specifications and unique detailed cutaway illustrations.

Respected world-wide, *AIR International* also provides regular reviews and analysis of national air arms, the world's airlines and aerospace companies. Future trends in aviation are addressed, as a historical subjects and included in each issue is the renowned up-to-the-minute survey of world-wide news events; military, commercial and industrial. *AIR International* captures all the latest news.

Monthly

This offer is limited to one magazine per household. Reply using the coupon, a photocopy or write to: Subscription Dept. (Free Copy), Key Publishing Ltd., PO Box 300, Stamford, Lincs., PE9 1NA, United Kingdom. Tel: (44) 01780 480404 Fax: 01780 757812. E-Mail: subs@keymags.demon.co.uk

http://www.keymags.co.uk

FREE MAGAZINES

For a limited period and while stocks last, you can claim a recent copy of any of these top-selling aviation magazines absolutely free. We'll also include a very special introductory offer to new subscribers. Can you afford to miss out? Simply complete the coupon and enclose two first class postage stamps (overseas readers please send four IRCs) to cover the post and packing and we'll forward you a copy by mail.

ue for money, some magazines stand out above the rest

AirForces MONTHLY

...getting to places where other military aviation cannot !

AirForces Monthly is devoted to 100% modern military aircraft. It has built up a formidable reputation by getting to places where other military aviation magazines only think about. *AirForces Monthly* has been there, taken photographs and captured world exclusive features long before others hear whispers.

AirForces Monthly's reputation is unrivalled world-wide.

Unbiased in its reporting on the world's air forces and their airpower, *AirForces Monthly* leads the way on potential "hotspot areas" and the airpower available to resolve certain situations. *AirForces Monthly* is constantly updating the strengths of air forces, their conflicts, weaponry, exercises, retirements, and cut-backs throughout the world. There's the latest write-offs, collisions, losses ad world-wide accident reports. Overall, an unrivalled mbination of up-to-the-minute news coverage, perb photography, and in-depth reporting from all er the globe makes *AirForces Monthly* e of the world's ading aviation magazines.

AIRLINERS — THE WORLD'S AIRLINE MAGAZINE

...full of facts on the world's airlines...

Published every other month, *Airliners* is the world's airline magazine. Dedicated to the ever changing and exciting world of airlines and airliners; the building of them, flying them and operating them. Published in the United States of America, *Airliners* carries world-wide reports on new airlines and the latest colour schemes plus a nostalgic look back at the history and preservation of airliners. Every issue is full to the brim with facts, figures, colour pictures and carries definitive articles on airlines of the world. There are in-depth features on airlines, their development, growth and in cases their demise. The latest technology and passenger comforts are tried and tested and fleet additions, sales and retirements are reported.

In addition, there are visits to major airports, news, trivia and much, much more. If you are interested in airliners then *Airliners* is the magazine for you.

SAMPLE ISSUE FORM

Name .... Address ....

.... Postcode .... Country ....

Please send me a copy of

AirForces Monthly ☐   Air International ☐   I enclose two first class stamps PER MAGAZINE ☐
Air Enthusiast ☐   Airliners ☐   I enclose four IRCs PER MAGAZINE ☐

Offer expires 30th November 1998 for UK readers and 31st December 1998 for overseas readers

Lancaster Data

A total of 7,377 Lancasters were built, including three prototypes, the majority (3,670) coming from the A V Roe works at Manchester and Yeadon. Production peaked in the second half of 1944 at which time an average of 250 aircraft were being delivered every month.

The production variants were:

Lancaster Mk.I - the initial production variant with Merlin XX, 22 or 24 engines.

Lancaster B.1 (Special) - modified to carry 12,000lb bomb.

Lancaster B.1 (FE) - tropicalised for Tiger Force ops in Far East.

Lancaster PR.1 - photo reconnaissance variant.

Lancaster Mk.1 (Western Union) - supplied to Aéronavale.

Lancaster Mk.II - with Bristol Hercules VI or XVI.

Lancaster Mk III - with Packard Merlin 28, 38 or 224.

Lancaster ASR.III - with Merlin 224, provision for airborne lifeboat.

Lancaster MR.III/GR.III - converted for maritime reconnaissance.

Lancaster IV - Avro 694, became Lincoln Mk.I.

Lancaster V - became Lincoln Mk.II.

Lancaster VI - with Merlin 85 or 87.

Lancaster Mk.VII/VII (FE) - built by Austin Motors, Martin top turret.

Lancaster Mk.VII (Western Union) - supplied to Aéronavale.

Lancaster Mk.X - built by Victory Aircraft, Canada.

The designations were somewhat variable in that, for example, the GR.III was also the GR.3 when the RAF abandoned the use of Roman numerals; likewise, the Mk.III easily became the B.III. Other designations, such as those given to the postwar RCAF Lancasters are covered in the appropriate articles within this magazine.

Inside the Lancaster

The BBMF's Lancaster I PA474 has all the standard crew stations, the only significant difference being the dual control arrangement for the pilots.

Pilot

Bomb Aimer

Flight Engineer

Navigator

Wireless Operator

Mid Upper Gunner

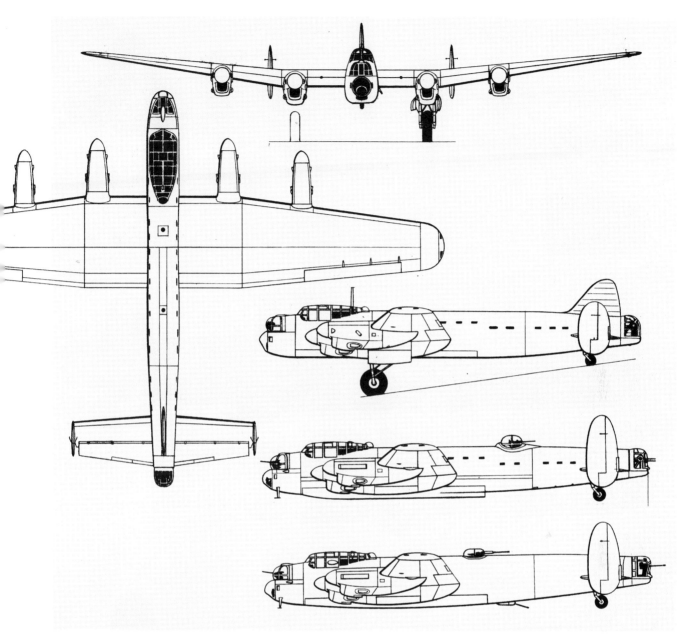

Rear Gunner (All FP - Duncan Cubitt)

The main 3-view shows the prototype complete with its central fin; the others show a production Mk.I with bomb doors for 8,000lb and a late production aircraft with B.17 dorsal turret, B.32 ventral turret and FN.82 rear turret. (FP Collection)

Lancaster Mk.I

Span -	102ft
Length -	69ft 6in
Crew -	7
Engines -	four Merlin XX, 22, 24
Max speed -	275 mph
Service ceiling -	19,000ft
First flight -	prototype, BT308, January 9, 1941
First flight -	production , L7527, October 31, 1941
Entry to service -	December 1941, 44 Squadron, RAF Waddington

Production summary

Prototypes	3	A V Roe
Mk.1	948	Metropolitan-Vickers
	911	Armstrong Whitworth
	890	A V Roe
	300	Vickers-Armstrongs
	235	Vickers
	150	Austin Motors
total Mk.1	3,434	
Mk.II	300	Armstrong Whitworth
Mk.III	2,780	A V Roe
	132	Metropolitan-Vickers
	118	Armstrong Whitworth
total Mk.III	3,030	
Mk.VII	180	Austin Motors
Mk.X	430	Victory Aircraft

By manufacturer the totals were:

A V Roe	3,673
Armstrong Whitworth	1,329
Metropolitan-Vickers	1,080
Vickers-Armstrongs	535
Austin Motors	330
Victory Aircraft	430

Lancaster Mk.III ED989 of 57 Squadron.

Lancaster Mk.VII NX611 showing 630 Squadron and 57 Squadron codes.

Lancaster Mk.III EE136 of 189 Squadron.

Lancaster B.I (Special) PB996 of 617 Squadron.

Lancaster Mk.I LL904 of 619 Squadron.

Lancaster GR.3 RE164 of No.1 School of Maritime Reconnaissance.

Lancaster MK.VII (FE) NX612 of 1689 Flight.

Lancaster MK.VII (Western Union) NX611 of Flotille 25.

Lancaster 10 of 107 Rescue Unit, RCAF.

(Artwork © Key Publishing/Pete West)

Medal group to Dennis Witt: Distinguished Service Order (DSO), Distinguished Flying Cross (DFC), Distinguished Flying Medal (DFM), 1939-45 Star, Aircrew Europe Star, Africa Star, Defence Medal, War Medal, General Service Medal (Malaya clasp), Coronation Medal EIIR. (FP - Duncan Cubitt)

Master Bomber

Graham Pitchfork details the operational career of Dennis Witt — from early operations with Whitleys through to Master Bomber on Lancasters.

DORSET-BORN DENNIS WITT started his long and distinguished career as an aircraft apprentice, arriving at Halton on January 20, 1931. Having enlisted as an instrument maker, he carried out his training at the Electrical and Wireless School at Cranwell. He graduated three years later as a Leading Aircraftman and spent the next two years serving on bomber squadrons gaining accelerated promotion to Corporal in August 1935. He was recommended for training as an airman pilot but he had to wait 18 months before commencing his flying training.

Dennis Witt reported to 9 Flying Training School in March 1937 and he gained his wings and promotion to Sergeant at Hullavington on October 23, following which he was posted as a bomber pilot to 10 Squadron based at Dishforth.

Initially, Witt flew as a second pilot and he took part in the Squadron's first operational sortie three days after the declaration of war when he dropped leaflets over the port of Lübeck. After more 'Nickel' sorties, the Whitleys were tasked in mid-December to carry out security patrols at night over the seaplane bases of Northern Germany and Witt flew sorties to Sylt, Borkum and Norderney. In February, new instructions came from Bomber Command tasking the Whitley squadrons to carry out reconnaissance sorties against the German transportation system.

After raids against the Luftwaffe-held airfield at Stavanger in Norway during April, the bombing war over the German mainland commenced as a direct reprisal for the indiscriminate bombing of Rotterdam. The 'Phoney War' was over but targets were restricted to those associated with the oil industry and the transportation system.

During his Whitley tour, Dennis Witt had earned a reputation as a captain who allowed

Dennis Witt started his flying career with Whitleys, progressing to Stirlings and then Lancasters.

nothing to deter him from his objectives. He had the rare distinction of never abandoning a sortie and he frequently remained over the target to obtain confirmation of his aiming point before commencing his bombing runs and, on many targets, he made numerous attacks. This was never more in evidence than during the RAF's first bombing raids on the Italian cities of Turin and Milan during August 1940 when many aircraft were forced to turn back. He reached Milan and circled the target until his bomb aimer had correctly identified the aiming point before releasing his bombs. He landed at Abingdon with the aircraft's tanks virtually dry. This raid was his 39th and final sortie with 10 Squadron. It came as no surprise a few weeks later when it was announced that he had been awarded the Distinguished Flying Medal. His Station Commander commented that "His integrity and devotion to duty is worthy of the highest praise". The Air Officer Commanding the Group added, "His work has been marked by the greatest zeal and courage and his devotion has been a consistent example to other members of the Squadron". Dennis Witt had established the pattern of excellence and courage that became the hallmark of his distinguished career. Two weeks after the announcement of his award he was commissioned as a Pilot Officer.

they crossed the English coast after being attacked and badly damaged over Hanover. Attacks against the German battle-cruiser Scharnhorst berthed in Brest were followed by daylight 'Circus' raids against targets in Northern France and it was during an attack against Bethune that his gunners shot down a Messerschmitt Me 109 fighter. After a visit to Berlin, the 'Big City', he led another daylight attack when most of the Stirlings were shot down but he pressed on against intense anti-aircraft fire and severely damaged the target.

to show the same courage, zeal and determination that he showed at the commencement of his operational tour in spite of the large number of sorties he has now completed". These outstanding citations speak for themselves. A week later, the Commander in Chief of Bomber Command approved the immediate award.

Duisberg was the target for seven Stirlings of 7 Squadron on the night of August 28, when they joined a mixed force of 118 bombers. Dennis Witt was one of the captains and it was his 64th bombing

Stirling I N3641 of 7 Squadron; Dennis Witt flew this aircraft on his first bombing sortie with the Squadron — Boulogne docks, February 15, 1941.

operation and the last of his second tour. Flying an old Stirling I (N3669), he dropped his five 1,000lb (454kg) and eight 500lb (227kg) bombs on the target and returned to base after one of the few routine sorties of his highly successful and dangerous tour on the first of the Stirling squadrons. He had deserved his rest. By the middle of 1941, Dennis Witt had established himself as one of the most experienced and outstanding bomber pilots in the Royal Air Force.

Having left 7 Squadron, Dennis Witt completed the Specialist Navigation Course before sailing for Canada where he was loaned to the Canadian Government to assist in the establishment of the British Commonwealth Air Training Plan. The plan, which was devised to train many thousands of young aircrew cadets, was one of the outstanding feats of organisation achieved during the war and Witt was heavily involved in establishing the early navigation schools.

In August 1942, he returned to the United Kingdom and was posted to Headquarters Bomber Command as a Squadron Leader to join the staff of the newly formed Pathfinder Force as a specialist navigator. With his unique experience of two bombing tours as a pilot, allied to his specialist navigation qualifications, he was an ideal candidate to be intimately involved in the early development of one of the most remarkable forces assembled during the war. He soon joined the Headquarters of Air Commodore

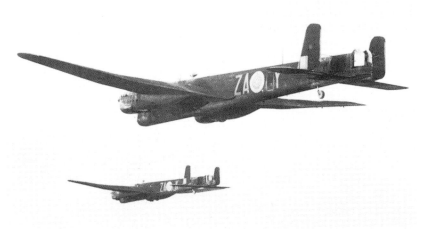

Witt completed a full bomber tour with 10 Squadron, flying many of the early Bomber Command night missions over Germany and Occupied Europe.

At the end of an arduous bomber tour, aircrew were normally posted to an Operational Training Unit (OTU) for a 'rest' as instructors. However, as Dennis Witt ended his time with 10 Squadron, the first of the four-engined bombers was entering service and experienced pilots were required to join the first Stirling squadron that was forming at Leeming. He was posted to join 7 Squadron which had been given the added responsibility of conducting proving trials before the Stirling was cleared for operations.

Witt flew on all the early Stirling operations. The enemy defences had increased significantly from the time of his Whitley days and losses were high. Witt frequently returned with 'flak' damage and on one occasion he and his crew had to bale out as

Immediately following the debrief of this operation, Witt's Squadron Commander submitted a glowing recommendation for the immediate award of the Distinguished Flying Cross, describing the circumstances of the attack and quoting details of his successful engagement with enemy fighters a few days earlier. He concluded his recommendation, "The success of this attack is attributed to the tenacity, skill and determination of this pilot. He is an outstanding captain who has gained signal success in operations against the enemy". His Station Commander commented on his "conspicuous courage, skill and devotion to duty", and Air Vice Marshal J Baldwin, who continued to fly on operations himself, added that "Flying Officer Witt continues

Lancaster of 635 Squadron — note the H2S radar bump under the fuselage and the AGLT (Automatic Gun Laying Turret) radar beneath the rear turret.

Don Bennett at 8 Group, based at Wyton, as the Group Training Inspector with the rank of acting Wing Commander. This marked the period when the Pathfinder techniques were being developed with the introduction of new navigation and bomb-aiming aids and target-marking equipment. Witt soon became restless sitting behind a desk and within a few months he commenced his efforts to return to operational flying.

Having completed two bomber tours, Dennis Witt could have completed the rest of the war in a comfortable ground appointment but that was not in his nature and he finally persuaded the Air Officer Commanding to allow him to return to a bomber squadron. The AOC insisted that he complete a series of refresher flying courses first and that he should attend the War Staff College Course where he could 'convert' those who doubted the value of the Pathfinder Force. He reverted to the rank of Squadron Leader and, in April 1944, he finally joined 635 Pathfinder Squadron equipped with Lancasters at Downham Market.

At that time, Bomber Command was formally committed to General Eisenhower for operations in support of Operation 'Overlord'. However, Witt initially had to complete his conversion training for Pathfinder operations before flying his first sortie just after D-Day. Immediately following the Allied landings in Normandy, the priority given to Bomber Command was to attack the German flying-bomb sites in the Pas de Calais area of Northern France.

Three days after the first flying-bomb landed on English soil, Dennis Witt took off on the night of June 16 from Downham Market in his Lancaster III (ND809) with 15 other Lancasters to bomb the 'construction works' at Rennescure. Cloud obscured the target but the 500lb bombs were dropped on the glow of the red TIs (Target Indicators).

Each crew joining a Pathfinder squadron flew their first few sorties as 'Supporters'. They carried only high explosive bombs and the aim was for them to arrive at zero hour in order to create the correct conditions for the incendiaries of the follow-up waves of bombers from the Main Force. On Witt's next sortie, the Squadron carried out the first attack directed against a V-1 site. Sixteen Squadron Lancasters were employed in the Supporter role against Coubronne, and Witt dropped his 1,000lb bombs on the red TIs which the Master Bomber had confirmed as accurate. Sadly, after directing an excellent attack, the Master Bomber failed to return.

Witt flew three more sorties in the bombing role against V-1 sites before Bomber Command was called on to bomb the city of Caen which was proving to be a major bottle-neck for the armies endeavouring to break-out of the Normandy bridge-head. On July 7, a barrage of 457 heavy bombers delivered almost 2,400 tons of bombs in the space of 38 minutes. The destruction of Caen was almost total and within a few days the army were able to make progress.

After two more attacks against V-1 sites, Witt flew his first sortie as an 'Illuminator' on July 14 when the Squadron attacked Revigny Marshalling Yard. White flares were dropped accurately from 12,000ft (3,650m)

Attack on the V-1 storage area at Trossy St Maxim, August 4, 1944.

but the 'Backers Up' failed to identify the target positively. To avoid casualties to the French civilian population in the surrounding built-up area, the Master Bomber finally called off the attack.

During the latter part of July, Bomber Command was given clearance to mount a number of attacks against German targets. Witt took his Lancaster to Kiel on July 23 and to Stuttgart the following night when 4,000lb (1,800kg) HC Minol bombs were dropped. The target was covered by a blanket of stratocumulus cloud at 5,000ft (1,500m) but a diffused glow from the red TIs was clearly visible. Flares were dropped for a 'Wanganui' sky-marker attack that achieved a good concentration, and the Master Bomber gave instructions to bomb the flares. Some crews reported seeing explosions in the target area and Witt, who was amongst the last to leave the area, reported that a good glow was clearly visible through the cloud. Four nights later 635 Squadron Lancasters attacked Hamburg with 2,000lb bombs. He was flying in the 'Blind Backer-up' role which involved going out with the main bomber stream and dropping further sky markers using the H2S radar. Night fighters were very active and over 7% of the bomber force was lost.

Early August marked a return to attacks on the Battle Area and the V-1 sites. On

completely obscured by smoke.

After the tragic loss of Bazalgette, Dennis Witt was made the Flight Commander and within a few days he acted as Master Bomber against a V-1 construction site at La Breteque. The OBOE-equipped Mosquitos had one of their rare failures when they put their markers down 6 miles (10km) from the aiming point. It took some time for this error to be realised and, in the meantime, the Deputy Master Bomber had backed up the errant red markers. Witt marked the correct target with his greens but he had great difficulty communicating this to the Main Force and it was estimated that only 25% of the Force attacked the correct target.

After a daylight attack on the railway centre at Lens, 635 Squadron made two attacks against the Opel Factory at Russelheim. This had been one of Germany's biggest automobile factories before the war but it had been developed as a military vehicle and aircraft components factory. The first raid on August 12 was moderately successful but two weeks later, a concentrated attack caused considerable damage. Dennis Witt led off the 635 Squadron force of 16 Lancasters. His bomb-aimer, Sqn Ldr P Lester identified the target visually following an accurate attack with hooded flares and he dropped his TIs and a 4,000lb (1,800kg)

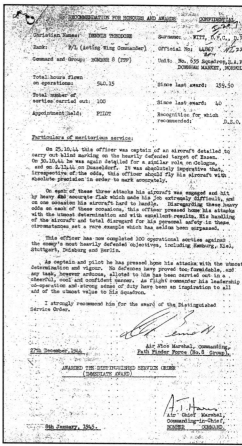

The recommendation for the award of the DSO was written by AVM Don Bennett, Commander of the Pathfinder Force.

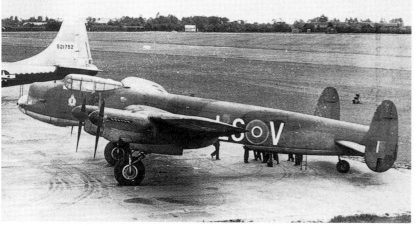

Lancaster B.1 (Special) PD131 of XV Squadron — flown by Dennis Witt on Operation 'Front Line' dropping 'Grand Slam' and 'Tallboy' bombs on concrete emplacements. (Norman Roberson)

August 4, 635 Squadron launched 14 aircraft on a daylight raid against the main V-1 stores area at Trossy St Maxim. Leading the 635 Squadron contingent was Squadron Leader Ian Bazalgette DFC who had been a Flight Commander since the Squadron's formation some months earlier and he had regularly carried out the duties of Master Bomber. Dennis Witt was flying as a 'Backer-up' with yellow TIs. These landed close to the red TIs which were to the right of the aiming point and the Master Bomber instructed the crews to bomb on the reds. The 'flak' was intense and the Master Bomber's aircraft was badly damaged but he continued to direct the attack until the target was

HC Minol bomb together. A good concentration was achieved and the fires from the target could be seen for over 100 miles (160km).

The following night the Squadron suffered three losses from a force of 16 when it attacked Kiel. Again, Witt carried a 4,000lb HC bomb together with 1,000lb armour-piercing bombs. He dropped his TIs using H2S but the raid was hampered by an effective smoke-screen; nevertheless the attack was acknowledged by the German authorities as 'a very serious raid' with extensive damage. Ten days after this successful offensive, Witt acted as a 'Blind Illuminator' on a very concentrated attack

against Frankfurt. Two Mosquitos from 608 Squadron, which shared Downham Market with 635, preceded the raid and dropped 'Window', which added to the confusion for the defences. It was three days before all the fires had been extinguished.

By mid-September, the Channel ports of Boulogne and Calais had failed to fall to the advancing armies and their non-availability to the Allies was causing major re-supply problems for Montgomery's troops who were advancing into Holland. The batteries of large calibre coastal guns were also still in operation and they posed a serious threat to Allied shipping. A number of major daylight raids were mounted and Witt acted as Deputy Master Bomber when 762 heavy bombers attacked Boulogne on September 17, and again when 646 attacked Calais on the 20th. The bombing was very concentrated and the German garrisons surrendered shortly afterwards. A week later, he acted as the Longstop Master Bomber on a daylight raid in the Calais area. Following these raids, Bomber Command was able to return to Germany in force for what the Commander in Chief of Bomber Command described as ' The Second Battle of the Ruhr'.

Dennis Witt was promoted again to Acting Wing Commander on October 7 and, with almost 30 Pathfinder operations, he was one of the most experienced captains in the Force. He flew all his remaining sorties in the Blind Marker role against the most heavily defended targets in Germany. The role of the Blind Marker was only undertaken by the most capable crews and their results determined the success or failure of the raid. They located the target on H2S and dropped the appropriate ground or sky markers, then remained in the target area to re-centre the attack if 'creep back' developed as the raid progressed. They also carried a heavy load of bombs to add to the weight of the Main Force.

After marking the target at Stuttgart with 'Wanganui' sky markers on October 19, Witt flew as a Blind Marker on a daylight raid to Essen on October 25. With almost complete cloud cover, it was once again necessary to use the 'Wanganui' sky markers and these were placed accurately. His Lancaster (PB585) was subjected to heavy anti-aircraft fire and the aircraft was damaged but he remained in the area to provide further marking. Considerable damage was inflicted on the giant Krupps industrial complex and much of the activity of this important target had to be dispersed to other sites. Five days later he dropped his markers over Cologne which suffered very heavy damage and, once again, he brought back a damaged bomber having been hit by flak over the heavily defended target.

Excellent weather conditions prevailed on November 2, when Dennis Witt and his crew carried out a 'Paramatta' ground marking attack with their green TIs on Düsseldorf after the OBOE-equipped Mosquitos had placed their red TIs close to the aiming point. For the third consecutive sortie, Witt's Lancaster suffered 'flak' damage but he remained in the target area to drop his 4,000lb HC and 1,000lb bombs. Over 900 heavy bombers attacked and this proved to be the last major raid against Düsseldorf which suffered extensive damage after this accurate attack.

After two successful blind marker sorties against Munster and Neuss, Dennis Witt and his long-standing crew rolled down the main runway at Downham Market at 1710 hours on November 30 in their recently repaired Z for Zebra (PB585) en-route to Duisberg. Complete cloud cover dictated a 'Wanganui' attack after the OBOE

Mosquitos had dropped their red TIs, which disappeared into cloud leaving a glow, thus indicating a good concentration. Five minutes later, Witt's green flares went down and the Main Force commenced their attack, which appeared to be well delivered.

Dennis Witt landed his Lancaster at 2120 hours and taxied back to the dispersal pan. As the engines gently windmilled to a stop, a small crowd gathered by the aircraft to greet the captain. He had returned safely from his 100th heavy-bomber sortie. He was informed that Air Vice Marshal Don Bennett, the Pathfinder leader, had decided that it was also to be his last and he was screened from any further operations. A few days later, he was

Dennis Witt, 3rd from right, and his crew pose with a XV Squadron Lancaster B.1 (Special). (All author unless stated)

awarded his Permanent Pathfinder Badge.

So ended the operational career of one of the most outstanding bomber pilots of the war. Just before he left for a flying instructors' course at the Empire Central Flying School, it was announced that an immediate award of the Distinguished Service Order had been approved. The recommendation, written personally by Air Vice Marshal Bennett, epitomises the dedication and gallantry of this officer.

Dennis Witt clearly led an outstanding crew who had flown with him throughout his tour. They too received well deserved awards, with the navigator, Sqn Ldr R W Coutts, receiving the Distinguished Flying Cross. There were Distinguished Flying Medals for the two air gunners, F/Sgts C Shaw and R S Stuart.

After completing a flying instructors' course, Witt flew on the Pathfinder Navigator Training Unit at Warboys until the end of the war when he reverted to the rank of

Squadron Leader. In March 1946 he assumed command of XV Squadron which was partially equipped with Lancaster B1 (Specials) originally used by 617 Squadron and modified to carry the 22,000lb 'Grand Slam' bombs. To reduce weight, the front and dorsal gun turrets had been removed.

During May, the Squadron took part in Operation 'Front Line' a combined exercise with USAAF B-29 Superfortresses. (The US authorities called the operation 'Ruby'.) This involved trials against the former U-boat pens at Farge near Bremen when the 'Grand Slam' and the smaller 12,000lb (5,400kg) 'Tallboy' bombs were dropped using the Mark XIV bombsight and the H2S radar bombing aid.

Dennis Witt remained in the Royal Air Force after the war and on May 8, 1954, he attended Lincoln Cathedral having been selected to represent the Officer Aircrew of Bomber Command at the dedication of the Bomber Command Memorial Window. At this most prestigious and moving ceremony in the cathedral that had been a beacon to the men of Bomber Command, he marched up the aisle behind his wartime boss, Marshal of the Royal Air Force Sir Arthur Harris. Surely there could have been no more worthy a representative of those unique men, the aircrew of Bomber Command, than Dennis Witt.

In February 1962, Group Captain Dennis Witt was selected to attend the prestigious senior officer's course at the NATO Defence College in Paris. Towards the end of the course he became ill and was admitted to the RAF Hospital at Uxbridge. On December 26, 1963, this modest and courageous ex-Halton apprentice who rose to be a Pathfinder Master Bomber, died.

The final word should rest with his Canadian navigator who flew with him on those early and extremely dangerous daylight raids in the Stirling and who wrote: "I can think of few others more worthy of tribute than Dennis Witt. He set a sterling example of skill and courage under fire and inspired great confidence in those around him. He deserves to be remembered."

(This article is an extract from Graham Pitchfork's highly successful book 'Men Behind the Medals'.)

RECCE TEST - win a £100 FlyPast bundle of aviation books.

The task is to identify the Lancasters shown below — but be careful as one or two other bombers have sneaked into the selection! Although we only ask you to identify the Lancasters, feel free to add the names of the other types if you wish (however, there's no extra prize for getting them right!)

There are plenty of photographs, 3-views and artwork in this issue to help you.

Send your answers to: Lancaster Recce Test, FlyPast, PO Box 100, Stamford, Lincs, PE9 1XQ. The closing date is January 1, 1999.

If no-one gets all the answers right then the prizes will go to those with the greatest number of correct answers. In the event of a tie, the winners will be drawn from all the correct entries.

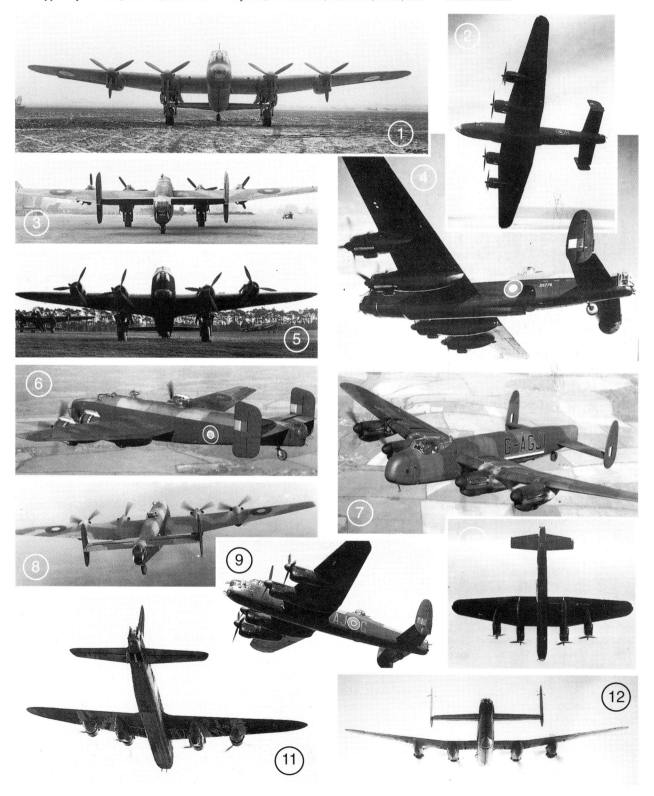

For Valour

Sqn Ldr John Nettleton VC with Sqn Ldr R G Whitehead DFC, 1942. (FP Collection)

The Victoria Cross (VC) was awarded on 32 occasions in World War Two to aircrew of the RAF and Commonwealth air forces; of the 19 which went to members of Bomber Command, ten were awarded to Lancaster aircrew.

this first Lancaster squadron. His citation reads:

"Squadron Leader Nettleton was the leader of one of two formations of six Lancasters detailed to deliver a low-level attack in daylight on the diesel engine factory at Augsburg in southern Germany on April 17, 1942. The enterprise was daring, the target of high military importance. To reach it and get back, some 1,000 miles had to be flown over hostile territory. Soon after crossing into enemy territory his formation was engaged by 25 to 30 fighters. A running fight ensued. His rear guns were out of action. One by one the aircraft of his formation were shot down until in the end only his and one other remained. The fighters were shaken off but the target was still far distant.

Though fired at from point-blank range, they stayed the course to drop their bombs true on the target. The second aircraft, hit by flak, burst into flames and crash-landed. The leading aircraft, though riddled with holes, flew safely back to base, the only one of the six to return. Squadron Leader Nettleton, who has successfully undertaken many other hazardous operations, displayed unflinching determination as well as leadership and valour of the highest order."

Nettleton subsequently served with 1661 HCU before returning to 44 Squadron as its OC in January 1943; he failed to return from a raid against Turin on the night of July 12/13, 1943.

May 16/17, 1943 - Wing Commander Guy Gibson VC, DSO* DFC* (No 617 Squadron)

Guy Penrose Gibson was commissioned into the RAF as a pilot in 1937, his first posting being to 83 Squadron, equipped with Hinds and then Hampdens, based at Scampton. Gibson took part in operations from the very first day of the war and had completed his first tour by September 1940. After a short tour as an instructor with Nos 14 and 16 OTUs he was posted to 29 Squadron based at Digby, flying Beaufighters as a night-fighter pilot until December 1941; he flew 100 operational sorties and was credited with three enemy aircraft destroyed.

Following a short period as an instructor with 51 OTU at Cranfield, Gibson returned to operational flying in April 1942 as Officer Commanding 106 Squadron at Coningsby, equipped with the Manchester and then the Lancaster. Having completed his tour of operations with No 106 Squadron he was asked to form and lead a special bomber squadron and thus became OC of 617 Squadron, leading the Dams Raid on the night of 16/17 May 1943. His citation reads:

"Under his inspiring leadership, this squadron

Lancaster of 44 Squadron - marked KM-B as the aircraft flown by Nettleton on the Augsburg raid. (Andy Thomas Collection)

April 17, 1942 - Squadron Leader John Nettleton VC (No 44 Squadron)

John Dering Nettleton was commissioned into the RAF as a pilot in December 1938 and flew tours with 207 Squadron, 98 Squadron, and 185 Squadron. In June 1941 he was posted to No 44 Squadron at Waddington as a Flight Commander on

There was formidable resistance to be faced. With great spirit and almost defenceless, he held his two remaining aircraft on their perilous course and after a long and arduous flight, mostly at only 50 feet above the ground, he brought them to Augsburg. Here anti-aircraft fire of great intensity and accuracy was encountered. The two aircraft came low over the roof tops.

has now executed one of the most devastating attacks of the war — the breaching of the Mohne and Eder dams. The task was fraught with danger and difficulty. Gibson personally made the initial attack on the Mohne Dam. Descending to within a few feet of the water and taking the full brunt of the anti-aircraft defences, he delivered his attack with great accuracy. Afterwards he circled very low for 30 minutes, drawing the enemy fire on himself in order to leave as free a run as possible to the

The Eder Dam on May 17, 1943. (Ken Delve Collection)

following aircraft which were attacking the dam in turn. Gibson then led the remainder of his force to the Eder Dam where, with complete disregard for his own safety, he repeated his tactics, and once more drew on himself the enemy fire so that the attack would be successfully developed. Wing Commander Gibson has completed 170 sorties. Throughout his operational career, prolonged exceptionally at his own request, he has shown leadership, determination and valour of the highest order."

Gibson was grounded shortly afterwards and took on various Staff appointments, although he managed to 'escape' from the office whenever he could to fly operational sorties. On the night of September 19, 1944, Gibson was flying a 627 Squadron Mosquito as Master Bomber against rail and industrial targets at Rheydt and Munchen-Gladbach. Eye witnesses reported seeing his aircraft in flames - it crashed at Steenbergen in Holland.

December 3, 1943 - Flight Lieutenant William Reid VC (No 61 Squadron)

William Reid joined the RAFVR in April 1941 and was posted to 61 Squadron at Syerston in September 1943. On December 3, 1943 he was en route to Düsseldorf. His citation reads:

"Shortly after crossing the Dutch coast, the pilot's windscreen was shattered by fire from a Messerschmitt 110. Owing to a

failure in the heating circuit, the rear gunner's hands were too cold for him to open fire immediately or to operate his microphone and so give warning of danger; but after a brief delay he managed to return the Messerschmitt's fire and it was driven off.

"During the fight with the Messerschmitt, Reid was wounded in the head, shoulders and hands. The elevator trimming tabs of the aircraft were damaged and it became difficult to control. The rear turret, too, was badly damaged and the communications system and compasses were put out of action. Reid ascertained that his crew were unscathed and, saying nothing about his own injuries, he continued his mission.

"Soon afterwards, the Lancaster was attacked by a Focke-Wulf 190. This time, the enemy's fire raked the bomber from stem to stern. The rear gunner replied with his only serviceable gun, but the state of his turret made accurate aiming impossible. The navigator was killed and the wireless operator fatally injured. The mid-upper turret was hit and the oxygen system put out of action. Reid was again wounded and the flight engineer, though hit in the forearm, supplied him with oxygen from a portable supply.

"Flight Lieutenant Reid refused to be turned from his objective and Düsseldorf was reached some 50 minutes later. He had memorised his course to the target and had continued in such a normal manner that the bomb aimer, who was cut off by the failure of the communications system, knew nothing of his captain's injuries or of the casualties to his comrades. Photographs show that when the bombs were released the aircraft was right over the centre of the target. Steering by the pole star and the moon, Reid then set course for home. He was growing weak from loss of blood. The emergency oxygen supply had given out. With the windscreen shattered, the cold was intense. He lapsed into semi-consciousness. The flight engineer, with some help from the bomb aimer, kept the Lancaster in the air despite heavy anti-aircraft fire over the Dutch coast.

"The North Sea crossing was accomplished. An airfield was sighted. The captain revived,

resumed control and made ready to land. Ground mist partially obscured the runway lights. The captain was also much bothered by blood from his head wound getting into his eyes. But he made a safe landing although the leg of the damaged undercarriage collapsed when the load came on.

Wounded in two attacks, without oxygen, suffering severely from cold, his navigator dead, his wireless operator fatally wounded, his aircraft crippled and defenceless, Flight Lieutenant Reid showed superb courage and leadership in penetrating a further 200 miles into enemy territory to attack one of the most strongly defended targets in Germany, every additional mile increasing the hazards of the long and perilous journey home. His tenacity and devotion to duty were beyond praise."

Bill Reid subsequently served with 617 Squadron, failing to return from a July 31, 1944, raid when his Lancaster was struck by a bomb from another Lancaster. Only two of the crew managed to escape and both were taken prisoner. Bill Reid remained a PoW to the end of the war.

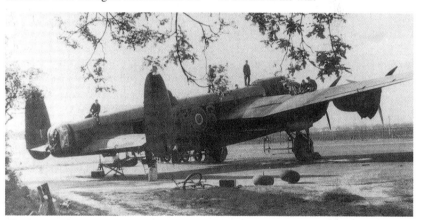

Norman Jackson was serving with 106 Squadron when he won his Victoria Cross. (Peter Green Collection)

April 26, 1944 - Sergeant Norman Jackson VC (No 106 Squadron)

Norman Cyril Jackson joined the RAF as an engine fitter but later became a flight engineer with 106 Squadron. In November 1943 the Squadron moved to Metheringham; on April 26 his Lancaster was part of the force attacking Schweinfurt. His citation reads:

"Bombs were dropped successfully and the aircraft was climbing out of the target area. Suddenly it was attacked by a fighter at about 20,000 feet. The captain took evading action at once, but the enemy secured many hits. A fire started near a petrol tank on the upper surface of the starboard wing, between the fuselage and the inner engine. Sergeant Jackson was thrown to the floor during the engagement. Wounds which he received from shell splinters in the right leg and shoulder were probably sustained at that time. Recovering himself, he remarked that he could deal with the fire on the wing and obtained his captain's permission to try to put out the flames. Pushing a hand fire extinguisher into

Norman Jackson with Gp Capt Leonard Cheshire. (Ken Delve Collection)

the top of his life-saving jacket, and clipping on his parachute pack, Jackson jettisoned the escape hatch above the pilot's head and started to climb out of the cockpit and back along the top of the fuselage to the starboard wing Before he could leave the fuselage his parachute pack opened and the whole canopy and rigging lines spilled into the cockpit. Undeterred, Jackson continued. The pilot, bomb aimer and navigator gathered the parachute together and held on to the rigging lines, paying them out as the airman crawled aft. Eventually he slipped and, falling from the fuselage to the starboard wing, grasped an air intake on the leading edge of the wing. He succeeded in clinging on but lost the extinguisher which was blown away.

"By this time the fire had spread rapidly. Jackson's face, hands and clothing were severely burnt. Unable to retain his hold he was swept through the flames and over the trailing edge of the wing, dragging his parachute behind. When last seen it was only partially inflated and was burning in a number of places. Realising that the fire could not be controlled, the captain gave the order to abandon the aircraft. Four of the remaining members of the crew landed safely; the captain and the rear gunner have not been accounted for. Sergeant Jackson was unable to control his descent and landed heavily. He sustained a broken ankle, his right eye was closed through burns and his hands were useless. These injuries, together with the wounds received earlier, reduced him to a pitiable state. At daybreak he crawled to the nearest village where he was taken prisoner. After ten months in hospital he made a good recovery, though his hands require further treatment and are only of limited use.

"This airman's attempts to extinguish the fire and save the aircraft and crew from falling into enemy hands was an act of outstanding gallantry. To venture outside, when travelling at 200 miles an hour at a great height and in intense cold, was an almost incredible feat. Had he succeeded in subduing the flames, there was little or no prospect of his regaining the cockpit. The spilling of his parachute and the risk of grave damage to its canopy reduced his chances of survival to a minimum. By his ready willingness to face these dangers he set an example of self-sacrifice which will ever be remembered."

Jackson became a Prisoner of War, being repatriated at the end of the war.

June 12, 1944 - Pilot Officer Andrew Mynarski VC (No 419 Squadron)

Andrew Charles Mynarski joined the RCAF as a wireless operator/air gunner and was posted to 9 Squadron in October 1943, moving to the Canadian 419 Squadron at Middleton St George the following April. As part of the post D-Day bombing campaign his Squadron took part in an attack on Cambrai on June 12. His citation reads:

"The aircraft was attacked from below and astern by an enemy fighter and ultimately came down in flames. As an immediate result of the attack, both port engines failed. Fire broke out between the mid-upper turret and the rear turret, as well as in the port wing. The flames soon became fierce and the captain ordered the crew to abandon the aircraft.

"Mynarski left his turret and went towards the escape hatch. He then saw the rear gunner was still in his turret and apparently unable to leave it. The turret was, in fact, immovable since the hydraulic gear had been put out of action when the port engines failed, and the manual gear had been broken by the gunner in an attempt to escape. Without hesitation Mynarski made his way through the flames in an endeavour to reach the turret and release the rear gunner. Whilst doing so, his parachute and his clothing, up to the waist, were set on fire. All his efforts to move the turret and free the gunner were in vain. Eventually the rear gunner clearly indicated to him that there was nothing more he could do and that he should

try and save his own life. Mynarski reluctantly went back through the flames to the escape hatch. There, as a last gesture to the trapped gunner, he turned towards him, stood to attention in his flaming clothing and saluted, before he jumped out of the aircraft. Mynarski's descent was seen by French people on the ground. Both his parachute and clothing were on fire. He was found eventually by the French, but was so severely burnt that he died from his injuries.

"The rear gunner had a miraculous escape when the aircraft crashed. He subsequently testified that, had Mynarski not attempted to save his comrade's life, he could have left the aircraft in safety and would, doubtless, have escaped death. Mynarski must have been fully aware that in trying to free the rear gunner he was almost certain to lose his own life. Despite this, with outstanding courage and complete disregard for his own safety, he went to the rescue. Willingly accepting the danger, Mynarski lost his life by a most conspicuous act of heroism which called for valour of the highest order."

August 4, 1944 - Squadron Leader Ian Bazalgette VC, DFC (No 635 Squadron)

Ian Willoughby Bazalgette was commissioned as a Second Lieutenant in the Royal Artillery but in 1941 transferred to the RAF Volunteer Reserve as a pilot. His first operational tour was with 115 Squadron flying Wellingtons and he was still with the Squadron when they converted to the Lancaster in early 1943, completing his

Andrew Mynarski was a Wireless Operator/Air Gunner with 419 Squadron (RCAF). (Ken Delve Collection)

tour in August. After an instructional tour with 20 OTU at Lossiemouth, Bazalgette returned to operational flying with the Pathfinders, joining 635 Squadron at Downham Market in April 1944. On August 4 that year the PFF marked the V-l storage site at Trossy St Maximin, Bazalgette was the captain of Lancaster ND811. His citation reads:

"When nearing the target his Lancaster came under heavy anti-aircraft fire; both starboard engines were put out of action and serious fires broke out in the fuselage, and the starboard main plane, and the bomb aimer was badly wounded. Despite the appalling conditions in his burning aircraft, he pressed on gallantly to the target, marking and

exploded and Bazalgette and his two comrades perished."

The deed was unrecorded until after the war when survivors of his crew returned to the UK. Their accounts of the sortie led to the award of a Victoria Cross to Squadron Leader Ian Bazalgette (LG August 17, 1945).

September 8, 1944 - Wing Commander Leonard Cheshire VC, DSO** DFC (No 617 Squadron)

Geoffrey Leonard Cheshire was commissioned as a pilot in the RAFVR in 1937 and by June 1940 was flying Whitleys with 102 Squadron, completing his first

"This officer began his operational career in June 1940. Against strongly defended targets, he soon displayed the courage and determination of an exceptional leader. He was always ready to accept extra risks to ensure success. At the end of his first tour of operational duty he immediately volunteered for a second. Again, he pressed home his attacks with the utmost gallantry. When he was posted for instructional duties in January 1942 he undertook four more operational missions. He started a third tour in August 1942 when he was given command of a squadron. He led the Squadron with outstanding skill on a number of missions before being appointed as a station commander.

Leonard Cheshire flew a number of operational tours, here with 35 Squadron. (Ken Delve Collection)

bombing it accurately. After the bombs had been dropped the Lancaster dived, practically out of control. By expert airmanship and great exertion Bazalgette regained control. However, the port inner engine then failed and the whole of the starboard main plane became a mass of flames. Bazalgette fought bravely to bring his aircraft and crew to safety; the mid-upper gunner was overcome by fumes. Bazalgette then ordered those of his crew who were able to leave by parachute to do so. He remained at the controls and attempted the almost hopeless task of landing the crippled and blazing aircraft in a last effort to save the wounded bomb aimer and helpless gunner. With superb skill, and taking great care to avoid a small French village nearby, he brought the aircraft down safely. Unfortunately, it then

tour the following January. He promptly volunteered for a second tour and was sent to join the Halifax-equipped 35 Squadron. Having completed his second tour of bomber operations, Cheshire was posted to No 1652 HCU as an instructor but in September 1942 returned to ops once more as OC 76 Squadron. April 1943 saw the 25-year-old Cheshire promoted to Group Captain to take command of RAF Marston Moor. However, he yearned to return to operational flying and so reverted to the rank of Wing Commander to become OC 617 Squadron at Woodhall Spa. Having flown his 100th operational sortie on July 6, 1944, Cheshire was withdrawn from operations and soon after this came the announcement of the award of the Victoria Cross to Cheshire (LC September 8, 1944). His citation reads:

"In October 1943 he undertook a fourth operational tour, relinquishing the rank of Group Captain at his own request so that he could again take part in operations. He immediately set to work as the pioneer of a new method of marking enemy targets involving very low flying. During his fourth tour Wing Commander Cheshire led his squadron personally on every occasion, always undertaking the most dangerous and difficult task of marking the target alone from a low level in the face of strong defences.

"Cheshire's cold and calculated acceptance of risks is exemplified by his conduct in an attack on Munich in April 1944. This was an experimental attack to test out the new method of target marking at low level against a heavily-defended target situated deep in enemy territory. He was obliged to follow, in bad weather, a direct route which took him over the defences of Augsburg and thereafter he was continuously under fire. As he reached the target, flares were being released by our high-flying aircraft and he was illuminated from above and below. All guns within range opened fire on him. Diving to 700 feet he dropped his markers with great precision and began to climb away. So blinding were the searchlights that he almost lost control. He then flew over the city at 1,000 feet to assess the accuracy of his work and direct other aircraft. His own was badly hit by shell fragments but he continued to fly over the target area until he was satisfied that he had done all in his power to ensure success. Eventually, when he set course for base, the task of disengaging himself from the defences proved even

flying Mosquitoes. By December 1944 he had flown over 100 operational sorties but rather than take a rest he stayed with the Squadron. On December 23, Palmer was Master Bomber for a raid against marshalling yards at Cologne, flying a 582 Squadron Lancaster. His citation reads:

"This officer has completed 110 bombing missions. Most of them involved deep penetration of heavily-defended territory; many were low-level 'marking' operations against vital targets; all were executed with tenacity, high courage and great accuracy. The finest example of his courage and determination was on December 23, 1944, when he led a formation of Lancasters to attack the marshalling yards at Cologne in daylight. He had the task of marking the target, and his formation had been ordered to bomb as soon as the bombs had gone from

January 1, 1945 - Flight Sergeant George Thompson VC (No 9 Squadron)

George Thompson joined the RAF as a wireless tradesman but transferred to flying duties as a wireless operator in 1943. He eventually joined 9 Squadron at Bardney in September 1944; on January 1 the following year his aircraft was involved in a daylight attack on the Dortmund-Ems Canal. His citation reads:

"The bombs had just been released when a heavy shell hit the aircraft in front of the mid-upper turret. Fire broke out and dense smoke filled the fuselage. The nose of the aircraft was then hit and an inrush of air, clearing the smoke, revealed a scene of utter devastation. Most of the Perspex screen of the nose compartment had been

Flight Sergeant George Thompson was with 9 Squadron in January 1945. (Peter Green Collection)

more hazardous than his approach. For a full 12 minutes after leaving the target area he was under withering fire, but he came safely through.

"Wing Commander Cheshire has now completed a total of 100 missions. In four years of fighting against the bitterest opposition he has maintained a record of outstanding personal achievement, placing himself invariably in the forefront of the battle. What he did in the Munich operation was typical of the careful planning, brilliant execution and contempt for danger which has established for Wing Commander Cheshire a reputation second to none in Bomber Command."

December 23, 1944 - Squadron Leader Robert Palmer VC DFC* (No 109 Squadron)

Robert Anthony Maurice Palmer joined the RAF as a sergeant pilot in 1939 and flew tours with 75 Squadron and 149 Squadron. After completing his first operational tour, he went to 20 OTU at Lossiemouth as an instructor. Commissioned in January 1942 he returned to operational flying with 109 Squadron at Warboys in January 1944,

his, the leading aircraft.

"The leader's duties during the final bombing run were exacting and demanded coolness and resolution. To achieve accuracy he would have to fly at an exact height and airspeed on a steady course, regardless of opposition. Some minutes before the target was reached, his aircraft came under heavy anti-aircraft fire, shells burst all around, two engines were set on fire and there were flames and smoke in the nose and the bomb bay. Enemy fighters now attacked in force. Palmer disdained the possibility of taking avoiding action. He knew that if he diverged the least bit from his course, he would be unable to utilise the special equipment to the best advantage.

"He was determined to complete the run and provide an accurate and easily seen aiming point for the other bombers. He ignored the double risk of fire and explosion in his aircraft and kept on. With his engines developing unequal power, an immense effort was needed to keep the damaged aircraft on a straight course. Nevertheless, he made a perfect approach and his bombs hit the target. His aircraft was last seen spiralling to earth in flames. Such was the strength of the opposition that more than half of the formation failed to return."

shot away, gaping holes had been torn in the canopy above the pilot's head, the inter-communications wiring had been severed, and there was a large hole in the floor of the aircraft. Bedding and other equipment were badly damaged or alight; one engine was on fire.

"Thompson saw that the gunner was unconscious in the blazing mid-upper turret. Without hesitation he went down the fuselage into the fire and exploding ammunition. He pulled the gunner from his turret and, edging his way round the hole in the floor, carried him away from the flames. With his bare hands, he extinguished the gunner's burning clothing. Thompson himself sustained serious burns on his face, hands and legs. Thompson then noticed that the rear turret was also on fire. Despite his own severe injuries he moved painfully to the rear of the fuselage where he found the rear gunner with his clothing alight, overcome by flames and fumes. A second time Thompson braved the flames. With great difficulty he extricated the helpless gunner and carried him clear. Again, he used his bare hands, already burnt, to beat out flames on a comrade's clothing

"Flight Sergeant Thompson, by now

the stalwart hero

almost exhausted, felt that his duty was not yet done. He must report the fate of the crew to the captain. He made the perilous journey back through the burning fuselage, clinging to the sides with his burnt hands to get across the hole in the floor. The flow of cold air caused him intense pain and frost-bite developed. So pitiful was his condition that his captain failed to recognise him. Still, his only concern was for the two gunners he had left in the rear of the aircraft. He was given such attention as was possible until a crash-landing was made some 40 minutes later.

"When the aircraft was hit, Flight Sergeant Thompson might have devoted his efforts to quelling the fire and so have contributed to his own safety. He preferred to go through the fire to succour his comrades. He knew that he would then be in no position to hear or heed any order which might be given to abandon the aircraft. He hazarded his own life in order to save the lives of others. Young in years (24 years old) and experience, his actions were those of a veteran.

"Three weeks later Flight Sergeant Thompson died of his injuries. One of the gunners unfortunately also died, but the other owes his life to the superb gallantry of Flight Sergeant Thompson, whose courage and self-sacrifice will ever be an inspiration to the Service."

February 23, 1945 - Captain Edwin Swales VC DFC (No 582 Squadron)

Edwin Swales trained as a pilot in the SAAF and was seconded to the RAF in August 1943, joining 582 Squadron at Little Staughton in mid-1944. On February 23, 1945, Swales was chosen as Master Bomber for a raid against the Pforzheim rail junction. His citation reads:

"As 'Master Bomber', he had the task of

Ted Swales and crew, February 1945.

July 1944 daylight mission over France, Swales flying 582 Squadron Lancaster 'P'. (Peter Green Collection)

locating the target area with precision and of giving aiming instructions to the main force of bombers following in his wake. Soon after he had reached the target area he was engaged by an enemy fighter and one of his engines was put out of action. His rear guns failed. His crippled aircraft was an easy prey to further attacks. Unperturbed, he carried on with his allotted task; clearly and precisely he issued aiming instructions to the main force. Meanwhile, the enemy

fighter closed the range and fired again. A second engine of Swale's aircraft was put out of action. Almost defenceless, he stayed over the target area issuing his aiming instructions until he was satisfied that the attack had achieved its purpose.

"It is now known that the attack was one of the most concentrated and successful of the war. Captain Swales did not, however, regard his mission as completed. His aircraft was damaged. Its speed had been so much

reduced that it could only with difficulty be kept in the air. The blind flying instruments were no longer working. Determined at all costs to prevent his aircraft and crew from falling into enemy hands, he set course for home. After an hour he flew into thin-layered cloud. He kept his course by skilful flying between the layers, but later heavy cloud and turbulent air conditions were met. The aircraft, by now over friendly territory, became more and more difficult to control; it was losing height steadily. Realising that the situation was desperate, Swales ordered his crew to bale out. Time was very short and it required all his exertions to keep the aircraft steady while each of his crew moved in turn to the escape hatch and parachuted to safety. Hardly had the last crew member jumped when the aircraft plunged to earth. Captain Swales was found dead at the controls. Intrepid in the attack, courageous in the face of danger, he did his duty to the last, giving his life that his comrades might live."

Lancaster of 107 Search and Rescue Unit. (Hugh Halliday)

Lancasters over Canada

Many a World War Two aircraft type became an object lesson in beating swords into ploughshares. Once the 'Cold War' developed, many such ploughshares were hastily reconverted to swords. Such was the case of the Avro Lancaster in RCAF postwar service, as Hugh A Halliday reports.

THERE WAS NO shortage of Lancasters in Canada in the summer of 1945. The last 25 manufactured by Victory Aircraft (Toronto) had never gone overseas, while no fewer than eight squadrons (some quickly converted from Halifaxes to Lancasters) had flown back to Canada. No 664 Wing was formed at Greenwood, Nova Scotia, the first step in preparing the RCAF for operations in the Pacific as part of 'Tiger Force'. The war's end, even before flying training began, led to disbandment of that formation. Air Vice-Marshal C R Slemon, the designated AOC of the RCAF component, reported to his new command, thanked the men for having volunteered, and wished them well in peacetime, all in a single day. Most of the Lancasters were placed in storage, pending final disposition.

A total of 229 Lancasters eventually passed through the RCAF inventory over the next 19 years. In many instances, their careers were brief; they wound up as scrap metal in 1947. Some were battle veterans from overseas with too much airframe time to make them attractive for postwar service. The first to go were KB721 and KB748 (both veterans of service with 419 Squadron and both converted to instructional airframes, August 1945). A happy exception was

Lancaster FM207 of 408 Squadron. (Andy Thomas Collection)

KB781 (veteran of wartime service with 428 Squadron) which was not scrapped until January 1956.

Adaptation and alteration of Lancasters began almost immediately after war's end. As of September 1945 the Test and

Development Establishment at Rockcliffe (Ottawa) experimented with propeller alcohol de-icers on KB739 — the first of many Lancaster modification trials over the years. This particular installation had been used previously on Mosquitos, a type widely flown at OTUs in Canada. The fact was that the Lancaster needed much modification before it could be put to domestic use. Avro Canada (successor to Victory Aircraft) did most of this work until 1951, when Fairey Aviation of Canada (Dartmouth, Nova Scotia) became prominent.

With one exception, all postwar RCAF Lancasters were Canadian-built Mark 10s, and they were variously designated according to their diverse roles and all modified to some degree to meet the requirements of their specialised tasks.

nose and tail turrets, sonobuoy capacity, rear-facing F.24 camera, extra fuel tanks, depth charges, radio and radar navigation aids.

Lancaster 10N — navigation trainer (unarmed); five modified of which four were named: FM206 'Northern Cross', FM208 'Polaris', FM211 'Zenith', KB826 'Orion' and KB986.

Lancaster 10O — engine test-bed; one only (FM209) modified by removal of two outer Merlins and replacement with two Orenda jet engines.

Lancaster 10P — photographic survey

America. When not flying in sub-Arctic conditions, it was visiting Victory Aircraft at Malton, near Toronto (where Canadian Lancaster production was centred) or taking part in public relations flights. EE182 occasionally flew to the United States on demonstration missions at major bases. Squadron Leader S O Partridge piloted the aircraft through much of this phase of its career, and checked out 84 American service and civilian pilots on the type, even without dual controls.

The first Lancasters pressed into peacetime

September 1949, 408 Squadron aircraft at Trenton. (Larry Mulberry)

service were KB884 and KB917, introduced into No 7 (Photographic) Wing, Rockcliffe. The RCAF was about to embark upon a project that had occupied much of its prewar resources — aerial mapping of the vast Canadian hinterland. Much had changed since 1939 — aircraft, cameras, navigational aids. More than anything else, however, the techniques of aerial survey had been altered by wartime experience. Prewar Bellanca and Northrop aircraft had photographed relatively small areas from altitudes of 5,000 to 7,000ft (1,500 to 2,100m). Lancasters and Mitchells could devour large tracts from 15,000 to 22,000ft (4,500 to 6,700m) using combinations of vertical and oblique cameras.

The photographic operations were conducted at first under the aegis of 7 Wing (later designated 22 Wing). Initially few Lancasters were used; the machines had to be adapted to their new (non-belligerent) roles and changes here might begat new problems requiring more tinkering. Removal of the rear turret, for example, required its replacement with 600lbs (270kg) of ballast. Unfortunately, this complicated handling when the aircraft were ferrying personnel, baggage and spares between bases. Early experience with 13 (later 413 Squadron) revealed alarming characteristics. One pilot reported having to apply full elevator trim and pushing the stick fully forward to maintain a standard landing approach.

404 Squadron's KB959 operating out of Greenwood, Nova Scotia. (National Aviation Museum)

These were:

Lancaster 10AR — specially adapted for Arctic reconnaissance (similar to Mk.10P with extended nose and rear observation windows). Three only (KB839, KB882, KB976).

Lancaster 10BR — maritime reconnaissance aircraft with added fuel capacity, radar torpedoes and depth charges.

Lancaster 10DC — two only (KB848, KB851) to carry two underwing Ryan Firebee recoverable target drones.

Lancaster 10MR and 10MP — maritime reconnaissance and patrol versions with

and reconnaissance, with no armament, trimet cameras, Fairchild F.224 or K.17B ordnance survey cameras, extra fuel, high and low level radio altimeters, and extensive navigational aids (LORAN, Rebecca).

Lancaster 10S — standard postwar bomber with mid-upper turret removed.

Lancaster 10U — unmodified wartime bomber.

The sole Mark 3 in Canadian service was EE182, which was brought to Canada in 1944 for 'winterization' trials and stayed on until March 1948 when it was scrapped. EE182 was widely viewed in wartime North

Technicians at Avro Canada work on an unidentified aircraft — was it one of those veterans that was quickly scrapped? (via Hugh Halliday)

Other defects had to be overcome, from camera lens fogging at altitude to navigational anomalies in the proximity of the North Magnetic Pole.

No 413 Squadron flew Lancasters only until the autumn of 1948, but a re-formed 408 Squadron operated 'Lancs' in the photographic and Arctic reconnaissance roles from January 1949 until the retirement of the type in April 1964. Some of the earliest photo work was also the most publicised. In July 1948 Flight Lieutenant C D Bennett and the crew of FM214 discovered themselves over land in Foxe Basin where only water had been previously charted. They had blundered upon two hitherto uncharted islands and thus added some 5,000 square miles (13,000km2) to Canadian territory.

The introduction of Lancasters into northern operations had many advantages. The safety associated with having four engines raised crew confidence and the type's potential endurance of 14 hours airborne permitted selection of alternative mapping or reconnaissance sites if weather proved

unfavourable in the primary area. Crew comfort (compared to Mitchells and Cansos) was also enhanced. On the other hand, undulating gravel northern runways wore out tyres and stressed undercarriages. The Packard Merlin 224 had to be changed every 300 hours, and it was not uncommon for Lancasters operating in the extended daylight of an Arctic summer to fly upwards of 400 hours a season. In 1949 alone, 408's eight Lancasters needed 62 Merlin changes in the field — 44 because of time-expired engines, five due to valve failures, and the balance attributable to assorted

mechanical problems.

No 408's mapping programme was considered one of the RCAF's finest postwar achievements, although it was certainly not unique to Canada. In many ways it resembled the work done by 82 Squadron (RAF) with Lancasters in Africa and 87 Squadron (RAAF) using Mosquitos in Australia. All such units employed navigational techniques that had been developed during the war, notably SHORAN (Short Range Aid to Navigation), formerly a blind-bombing device relying on air transportable beacons used to measure distances between two or three points, refining photographing along straight flight lines.

Nevertheless, Lancaster 10Ps also participated in tasks unlike any conducted by other Commonwealth countries. Most were conventional, but on August 14, 1948, FM218 (413 Squadron) figured in a rare piece of high drama. From Goose Bay it was 'scrambled' when a TCA North Star, en route from Britain, reported a double engine failure. The 'Lanc' rendezvoused with the airliner one hour after take-off and provided close escort back to Goose Bay.

Photographic work was essentially a summer operation. Each spring, until 1957, the 10Ps left Rockcliffe (home of the RCAF's Photo Establishment) and set up detachments across the country. For much of the time No 408 was a self-contained unit operating Lancasters, Dakotas, Cansos and Norsemen (the latter replaced in 1953 by Otters). The core work was done by the 'Lancs'; the other types provided logistical support. At the conclusion of each summer, the 'birds' returned to Rockcliffe to evaluate

The postwar RCAF Lancasters were amongst the most colourful — with silver finish and a variety of coloured bands. (National Aviation Museum)

results and prepare for the next photographic season. At such times the Lancasters became available for Arctic exercises held in conjunction with the army and with other RCAF units. Thus, in February 1950, three Lancasters were based at Whitehorse, Yukon Territory, for Exercise 'Sweetbriar', photographing 'enemy' positions and simulating bombing attacks. The 11-day operation taxed the ingenuity of groundcrews; the Lancaster was never an easy aircraft to maintain under Arctic conditions.

In October 1951, No 408 took atmospheric readings to help monitor Soviet atomic testing and then expanded into the realm of ice reconnaissance. Concern for Arctic defences heightened in 1954, when the unit commenced photographing a strip 40 miles (64km) wide, coast to coast, in preparation for the Mid-Canada Line of radar bases; this was completed in 1955. Also in 1954, 408 Squadron located and photographed Russian research camps established on floating ice islands. Some crews even took Russian language training, ostensibly in anticipation of forced-landings close to the stations but also to monitor simple radio transmissions. This work continued until 1964, when retirement of the 'Lancs' deprived No 408 of its long-range capability.

For much of its survey history, No 408 was commanded by Wing Commander J G Showler. The postwar RCAF was bound by a very restrictive policy governing honours and awards, but in 1958 his contributions (and that of his unit) were recognised by the award of the Trans-Canada Trophy (also known as the McKee Trophy) for extensive services to Canadian flying. In 1973 Showler was inducted into the Canadian Aviation Hall of Fame.

Particularly interesting work was performed in February and April 1962 as part of Operation 'Tirec II'. Four types of aircraft (No 408's Lancasters included) photographed an area from different heights. The purpose was to resolve difficulties that affected the new generation of photographic satellites in distinguishing between cloud, ice and snow. The realm of aerial survey and reconnaissance was being revolutionised at the very outset of the space age.

The onset of the 'Cold War' did not immediately affect Lancaster deployment in Canada; the formation of NATO in April 1949 had a greater impact. Concern for a possible Soviet submarine threat led to the formation of three maritime reconnaissance squadrons. The first — No 405 — formed at Greenwood on March 31, 1950; it operated Lancasters until November 1955 when the type was finally superseded by the Lockheed Neptune. No 404 Squadron was formed at Greenwood in April 1951 and flew Lancasters until September 1955 (again, Neptunes replaced 'Lancs') while 407 Squadron was formed at Comox, British Columbia, in July 1952, operating Lancasters until May 1959 (Neptune replacement had begun 13 months earlier).

Retrieval of Lancasters from storage and modification to the maritime reconnaissance role may well have been rushed, at least in the case of 405 Squadron (the first such unit 'on the beat'). Engine failures were frequent, often at remote places. On August 19, 1950, for example, FM221, had both port engines fail on final approach to Resolute Bay and crashed just short of the runway

One of the Firebee test-beds — designated Lancaster 10DC; two aircraft were modified to carry Ryan Firebee drones.

(fortunately with only one injury).

On the other hand, the most publicised postwar RCAF Lancaster accident had nothing to do with technical problems. On July 31, 1950, KB965 was detailed to drop two batches of supplies to the weather station at Alert (northern Ellesmere Island). One parachute caught on the port elevator and fouled the controls. There was no room to recover (the drop was being conducted at 1,000ft (300m]) and the aircraft crashed, killing W/C D T French and seven others (including two civilian observers). Other tragic Lancaster accidents subsequently involved FM102 (404 Squadron, crashed July 22, 1952, following collision with a Vampire - seven killed, including the fighter pilot); KB914 (405 Squadron, crashed in Labrador, February 1, 1952 - six killed); KB940 (407 Squadron, November 24, 1952 - eight killed including one civilian); KB966 (103 Search and Rescue Unit, Greenwood, April 20, 1953 - six killed); and KB995 (407 Squadron, May 26, 1953 - ten killed transporting spares to a 'Lanc' grounded in California).

Lancaster squadrons on maritime

The Lancaster was phased out of RCAF service in a ceremony at Downsview in April 1964. (Larry Milberry)

In Training Command colours, 407 Squadron's FM219 on a visit to Winnipeg in September 1961. (National Aviation Museum)

reconnaissance and ice patrols faced a variety of climates. Crews on the Atlantic coast might find themselves operating in Greenland, where fierce winds were known to blow aircraft out of their chocks and only a bulldozer could haul them back into place. By way of compensation, the same crews might shortly afterwards be engaged in joint exercises with British or American forces around Bermuda; Pacific coast crews, following detached duties on Arctic reconnaissance, might be sent to California for similar manoeuvres. At one time or another, all three maritime reconnaissance squadrons sent substantial Lancaster detachments to Britain to train alongside Coastal Command units; stations like St Eval or Londonderry sometimes had upwards to 35 RAF and RCAF Lancasters present, reminding some veterans of Bomber Command bases in 1945. Commanding Officers shamelessly used the type's fame for public relations and indoctrination of service pride. On February 21, 1958, 407 Squadron mobilised 12 Lancasters for a flypast on the departure of a popular base commanding officer. The same unit flew its last (highly publicised) Lancaster sortie with FM219 on May 12, 1959; the entire crew had served on type with Bomber Command.

Photographic and maritime patrol Lancasters were occasionally diverted to mercy missions,

such as evacuation of sick Eskimos from northern communities. However, search and rescue was the principal task of specialist flights across the country employing a variety of aircraft (Cansos, Dakotas, Lancasters, and eventually helicopters). Mercy and SAR flights were sometimes dramatic but most were routine affairs, undertaken with cool professionalism. Occasionally an incident stands out from the official record by virtue of courage displayed or peculiar circumstances.

The latter category includes an incident on October 10, 1954, when FM213 (107 Rescue Unit, Torbay, Newfoundland) was detailed to drop plasma at night to a vessel. The pilot (Flying Officer J K Vincer) made a test pass, had a hang-up on the second pass, and released the package on the third. His accuracy was phenomenal, for although the plasma was not recovered, the parachute and a marine marker were recovered on the deck of the ship. The following day, Flying Officer J P Davies (FM104) found the ship in zero visibility and made another plasma drop. This time the package (again delivered by a parachute with a marine marker) was retrieved from the sea by a lifeboat.

The two Firebee-toting Lancasters were part of an armament testing and development programme relating to the CF-100 Mark 6 (which did not progress beyond two prototypes). The work, directed by the

RCAF's Central Experimental and Proving Establishment, moved at a 'glacial pace' from June 1955 to February 1957.

Another unusual aircraft was FM209, modified to take two Orenda jet engines in lieu of the two outer Merlins. The first flight was on July 13, 1950, the Mk.10O logged some 500 hours from then·until July 1954, often using the Orendas alone. It was burned in a hangar fire at Malton.

On April 8, 1964, the Lancaster was ceremoniously retired from RCAF service at Station Downsview (Toronto). FM104 (ex-107 Rescue Unit) and KB976 were overflown by KB882 (the latter two ex-408 Squadron). These and a few surviving machines were speedily despatched to new duties as static display machines.

Before closing, reference must be made to RCAF Lancasters that ended up on the Canadian civil register: FM222 (CF-IMF), KB907 (CF-IMG) and KB909 (CF-IMH) were sold to Spartan Air Surveys of Ottawa for use as photographic aircraft; KB976 became a water bomber (CF-TQC) before sale to the Strathallan Collection as G-BCOH; CF-GBA (ex-TW870) was a former RAF Lancaster that had no RCAF connection. Its story is recounted in 'Air Transport in Canada', a two-volume work by Larry Milberry (Canav Books, Toronto).

Spartan Air Surveys acquired three Lancasters for use as photo survey aircraft.

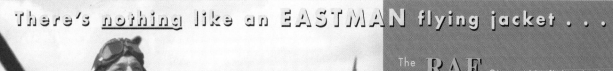 

THE BEST AVIATION ON VIDEO

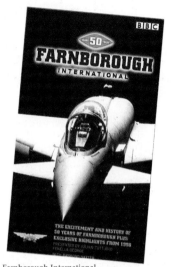

Flying Legend 1998
Duxford's Flying Legends show is firmly established as Europe's top display of vintage aircraft. There are no jets - just the drone of piston engines.
There are Spitfires of course - ten of them in this show. Alongside British rarities like the Hind, Gladiator, Blenhim and Lancaster, American air power is strongly featured. On US Independance Day come brilliant displays from the Mustang, Kittyhawk and King Cobra. There's a Navy "cats' chorus' of Tigercat, Bearcat, Hellcat and Wildcat and an appearance from the first Constellation to visit Britain for more than 20 years.
The programme also features the last pictures of Duxford's Catalina before its tragic accident in the Solent. 82 mins. £12.99

Farnborough International
The BBC "The Air Show" team presents the official video from Farnborough International, which for fifty years has been one of the world's premier aviation events. Expert view, analysis of the performance of the world's most powerful aircraft as they are put through their paces - aircraft which are often pitted in real combat years down the line. But it's not just fast jets; Farnborough is also the shop-window for new generations of airliners which each year shrink the world just a little more.
This video brings to life all the news and latest ideas which will change the face of civil, military and recreational flying for ever - premier coverage of the year's greatest aviation show.
73 mins. approx £14.99

British Airshows '98
All the biggest and best shows are included on this extra-length tape, as well as all the top displays. Relive the spectacular RAF 80th Anniversary celebrations at Fairford, marvel at stunning routines by the MiG-29 Fulcrum, Saab Viggen, Red Arrows, B-1B Lancer, Spitfires and a nine Sea Harrier formation - and witness the UK debuts of the majestic Berlin airlift C-54 Skymaster and the RAF's new Hercules C-130J.
A superb permanent record of an outstanding airshow season!
125 mins approx. £12.99

Spitfire '98
In 1938 the RAF took delivery of its first Spitfire at Duxford in Cambridgeshire. On May 2nd-3rd, 1998 the Imperial war Museum staged a spectacular air show to mark the aircraft's Diamond Jubilee. No fewer than 22 Spitfires were present with up to 16 flying in formation over the famous Battle of Britain airfield. Not since World War II has Britain seen such a pageant of these historic fighters - the turnout easily surpassing Duxford's successful Spitfire show of 1996
Spitfire '98 is a present day tribute to Britian's best loved aircraft. 75 mins £12.99

Farnborough 50's and 60's
During the 1950's, Britain led the world in aircraft design and the Farnborough Airshow was a yearly parade of the very British aviation had to offer. At every show throughout two decades, spectacular new fighters, bombers and airliners were unveiled to the world - Vulcan, Valiant and Victor V-bombers, the Javelin and Swift Fighters, the P-1 Lightning prototype, Comet Brabazon and VC10 airliners and the world-beating Concord supersonic airliner. 140 mins £12.99

German Jet Fighters
In 1944, Hitler ordered the full-scale production of, what he called the "Miracle Weapon". As a result, the first Jet Fighters were unleashed on the world. The potentially devastating ME262 and Arado 234 were underdeveloped and their moderate successes could not prevent the desperate situation which resulted in the introduction of the dangerous ME163 'Komet' and the disastrous Heinkel HE162 the 'Peoples Defender', more dangerous to its pilot than the enemy.
52 mins £12.99

The Royal International Air Tattoo 1998
The Royal International Air Tattoo, the world's biggest military airshow, hosts a spectacular tribute in celebration of The Royal Air Force's 80th Anniversary.The airshow salutes the 50th Anniversary of the Berlin Airlift including memorable film footage of a Lockheed Constellation, the immaculately restored South African Airways DC-4 Skymaster and supporting DC-3 Dakotas. Other highlights include 'SKYWATCH 98' - offering a fascinating insight into the world of surveillance and reconnaissance.
88 mins approx. £14.99

Bomber Command: Reaping The Whirlwind
This video sets the record straight. With extensive use of wartime film footage, it traces the story of RAF Bomber Command from the earliest missions dropping leaflets on occupied Poland to the massive raids on the German industrial heartland. This unique video also a look behind the scenes at Bomber Command briefings and debriefings and at the lives of the aircrew between missions with rare archive film, as well as dramatic footage of Lancasters, Wellingtons, Bostons and many other aircraft in action.
54 mins. £12.99

Paris Airshow '97
The Paris Airshow attracted more than 130,000 visitors with 1,700 trade exhibitors from 42 countries. Many of the 200 aircraft on show took part in the daily flying display. The video features two versions of the French Rafale fighter, the Mirage 2000, and a dual display of Eurofighters. From Russia there's the unusual Sukhoi SU-37 fighter with trust vectoring. 63 mins £12.99

Mildenhall Air Fete '98
Mildenhall's annual Air Fete means only one thing - fast and furious action. 10 countries provided fast jets, majestic transports, powerful helicopters and great aerobatic teams. At the forefront were some terrific displays - the USAF F-15C making its only showing this year and flying formation with Second World War Mustangs! The immense C-17 Globemaster transport shows how it handles like a fighter. The wild and wonderful Turkish Stars bring their NF-5A Freedom Fighters and put on a Stunning show. 60 mins £12.99

Classic Aeroplanes in Australia
Australia has one of the most varied collections of classic aeroplanes in the world. There are types of most of the great piston engined fighter aircraft of World War Two, as well as jets from former Warsaw Pact countries and a good selection of pre-war civilian types. Aircraft featured are CAC Boomerang, Sabre, Mustang, Sea Fury, T28 Trojan, Harvard, Cessna A37, PZL Iskra and MiG UTI. 60 mins. £12.99

Golden Air Tattoo
Nellis Air Force Base Las Vegas, Nevada April 25-26 1997
In April 1997, the United States Air Force (USAF) celebrated its official 50th anniversary with an unprecedented display of air power past and present at Nellis Air Force Base in Las Vegas, Nevada. A vast range of combat aircraft took to the air in what was undoubtedly one of the greatest air shows of all time, from veterans of the First World War to the very latest strike aircraft. 120 mins £12.99

FRENCH CONNECTIONS

Ken Ellis describes the Aéronavale Lancasters and their legacy.

With the trolley 'ack' supplying the vital spark, all four engines of the Lincolnshire Aviation Heritage's NX611 spring to life for the first time, July 1995. To port, she carries the colours of 'DX-C' Just Jane of 57 Squadron while on the starboard side is 'LE-C' of 630 Squadron, thereby representing the two East Kirkby Lanc units. (FP - Robert Rudhall)

BY FAR AND AWAY the largest source of today's extant Lancasters was the Royal Canadian Air Force. It might well be assumed that the next largest element must have come from the RAF. Not so, four of the survivors came from an oft-forgotten operator of the Lanc, the French naval air arm, the Aéronavale. (For the statisticians among the readers, the other survivors were sourced as follows: two from Britain, R5868 from the RAF and PA474 from the College of Aeronautics; then W4783 which came from Royal Australian Air Force charge.)

It is ironic that of the four Gallic survivors, only one is to be found in France and that machine came 'home' only as an afterthought. It was salvaged from the jungle on Wallis Island, north of Fiji in Polynesia, two decades after the other three had flown to new homes.

Like several other nations — Britain among them — France found herself with a postwar 'gap' in terms of long-range maritime patrol. Her commitments were not confined to France itself, but to a wide range of colonies and dependencies, particularly in Africa and in South East Asia. The ultimate answer lay in the Lockheed P2V Neptune, but that would be in the latter half of the 1950s.

With funding from the Western Union, via the Brussels Treaty Organisation, the offer

of 54 reworked Lancasters from the Avro facilities at Woodford and Langar was therefore very welcome. With the Lancs, France could meet the needs of maritime patrol, general reconnaissance and search and rescue (SAR) across the globe. The Western Union was formalised into the Western European Union in May 1955 and still exists, elements of the diplomatic and military missions to the former Yugoslavia being carried out as a function of the WEU.

From early 1951 to early 1953 France accepted the 54 Lancs, comprising 32 Mk.Is

and 22 Mk.VIIs. The aircraft received serial numbers prefixed with 'WU' from 1 to 54 in approximate order of delivery.

Work on the 54 involved inspect and repair where necessary, repainting and refinishing. To convert the bombers to their new role, the installation of an air-to-surface vessel (ASV) radar under the rear fuselage in a transparent fairing, long-range tanks, additional windows in the rear fuselage for observation, air-droppable lifeboat pick-up points (this option is thought not to have been used in 'anger') and fitting a

A follow-up delivery to the 54 Western Union Lancs comprised five examples reconditioned in late 1953 for special duties. FCL01, wearing high-visibility SAR markings served the RAF as RT693 with the Empire Air Navigation School and then the Central Navigation School at Shawbury. She was retired to Langar for rework on August 14, 1952, being test flown with the 'B Condition' markings G-11-72. (MAP)

Lovely air-to-air portrait of WU01, the first Western Union Lanc to be handed over to the Aéronavale, on December 7, 1951. The sortie was almost certainly out of St Eval, Cornwall, while French pilots worked up on the type. (Author's collection)

In 1958, three 25F Lancasters visited Durban, South Africa, to refuel after a flight from Madagascar, on their way home to their base at Lann-Bihoué in France. Among the three was WU15 which is today preserved in taxiable condition at East Kirkby. (Vic Pierson - Author's collection)

large chute under the rear turret for the dropping of life rafts, supplies, etc, was undertaken. The nose and rear turrets did not carry armament and were for observation purposes only.

A second order for Lancasters was placed in December 1953 for five aircraft for SAR and special duties. All Mk.VIIs, they were processed at Langar and given the serial numbers FCL01 to '05.

Crew conversion training was initially carried out at St Eval, Cornwall, then the home of the RAF's last remaining maritime Lancaster units. RAF Coastal Command was busy training up and accepting the Neptune which the RAF was to operate as a stop-gap between the Lancaster and the arrival in force of the Avro Shackleton.

The operational Aéronavale units were to fly the Lanc: Flottille 2F at Port Lyautey in Morocco; 10F at Lann-Bihoué in Brittany and 11F at Lartigue in Algeria. Additionally seven Escadrilles de Servitude used the type for training, general duties and SAR missions. These were: 4S in Tunisia, 5S in Algeria, 9S at Lann-Bihoué, 10S at St Raphael in the south of France and 52S, 55S and 56S in Morocco.

The rework by Avros saw the Lancs painted up in overall dark navy blue with white lettering and the attractive Aéronavale roundel and fin flash with anchor overlay. As time went on, the 'WU' prefix to their serials was dropped, with just the numerals remaining. Many aircraft also carried single letter codes in white on the fin and/or behind the trailing edge of the wing. These codes provided the 'last one' of their radio call-signs — for example, WU15 while in service with 55S at Agadir, Morocco, was 'F-YDOA' and carried 'A' on the fin accordingly.

By 1962 the only 'operational' unit flying the Lanc was 9S based at Tontouta in New Caledonia on general duties and SAR work. They had three Lancasters on strength from 1957 (Nos 16, 27 and 41) flying in overall

Among the three Durban visitors in 1958 was Mk.I WU28 (formerly TW648). Delivered to the Aéronavale on November 28, 1952, this was probably the last major sortie for this Lanc, as she was struck off charge in December 1958. (Vic Pierson - Author's collection)

white tropical colours with black spinners and black elements to the engine nacelles — perhaps to hide the oil and smoke stains! On odd examples the underwings were also painted black.

Wherever the Lancs were in the world, major servicing and equipment installation was undertaken by contractor Union de Transport Aerien (UTA) at Le Bourget, near Paris. In 1962 UTA undertook the last overhauls of Aéronavale Lancasters, preparing Nos 13, 15, 16 and 21 for service with 9S. These were also painted in the tropical white and used parts from their predecessors to keep them going.

During their service career, the Aéronavale lost 13 Lancs in accidents or crashes. Most of the fleet was withdrawn and scrapped with the arrival of the Neptunes in 1958-1959. Others served on with the Escadrilles de Servitude until they too gave up their Lancasters in 1961-1962, with a variety of types, including equally venerable Douglas C-47s, taking up the gauntlet.

It fell to 9S in New Caledonia to be the last French unit to operate Lancasters, giving them up operationally in 1964. Replacing the Lancs

NX611 on display at the gate of RAF Scampton, January 1984, with both 'Tallboy' and 'Upkeep' weapons in the foreground. (FP - Duncan Cubitt)

were Douglas C-54 Skymasters. France shares with Canada the laurel of the last 'operational' flights of the type — 408 Squadron, RCAF, withdrawing its last examples in March 1964 at Rockcliffe, Ontario.

Lancaster No.15 was the last to retire, perhaps its last major mission being to act as crew ferry to No.13 when it was delivered to New Zealand in April 1964 for preservation. No.15 (the redoubtable NX611) was struck off Aéronavale charge in August 1964, by that time she had clocked up around 2,200 hours of flying time.

The French authorities were well aware of the heritage and the meaning of their Lancasters and were determined to help them find new homes. First of the final 9S aircraft to retire was No.16 (the former NX622). In December 1962 she was ferried from Tontouta to Perth, Western Australia, and put on display to raise funds for the RAAF Association. She then moved to the RAAF Association Heritage Museum of Western Australia at Bull Creek, near Perth. Thankfully in 1983 sufficient funds were available to put the Lanc inside a new display hangar.

Thought taken at Bankstown, NSW, in August 1964, WU15 awaits the ferry flight to the UK for her new life with the Historic Aircraft Preservation Society. Sharing the ramp is Lockheed Hudson VH-AGX of Adastra Aerial Surveys which is also extant, in Victoria, awaiting restoration. (Author's collection)

Aéronavale Survivors				
WU	WU13	WU15	WU16	WU21
Mk	VII	VII	VII	VII
RAF Serial	NX665	NX611	NX622	NX664
Reconditioned at	Woodford	Woodford	Woodford	Woodford
To France	May 23, 1952	Jun 4, 1952	Jun 18, 1952	Aug 1952
Last Unit	9S	9S	9S	9S
Withdrawn	Apr 1964	Aug 1964	Dec 1962	Jan 21, 1963*
To Preservation	Apr 15, 1964	May 13, 1965	Dec 1962	1984
Current Location	MoTTaSH	LAHC	RAAFA	Musée de l'Air
	Auckland	East Kirkby	Bull Creek	Le Bourget
	New Zealand	UK	Australia	France
Status	Static,	Taxiable,	Static,	Restoration,

* Crashed on landing on Matu Utu, the Wallis Islands and later stripped for spares.

By the early 1960s the remaining Lanc fleet had taken on a tropical overall white colour scheme. WU13 kept the underwings black. This aircraft is preserved in New Zealand. (MAP)

To keep the dwindling fleet of Lancasters going, contractors Union de Transport Aerien stripped several examples for spares at Le Bourget and the hulks were used by the fire crews. Two Lancs undergoing a slow death, 1965. (Bill Hale — Author's collection)

Enthusiasts abandon their bicycles to admire NX611, now named Guy Gibson and camouflaged at Biggin Hill in 1966 or 1967. The codes 'HA-P' denote its custodians, but fortuitously were used by 218 Squadron Lancs in 1944 and 1945. (Author's collection)

As already mentioned, No.15 acted as escort to No.13 (the former NX665) which was flown to Whenuapai on April 15, 1964, having been presented to the Museum of Transport and Technology at Auckland. The Lanc arrived at its new home by road on May 4, 1964, but it was not to be until the late 1980s that this Lancaster was moved into a new display hangar in what has become the ponderously-worded Museum of Transport, Technology and Social History (MoTTaSH).

Following appeals from the UK-based Historic Aircraft Preservation Society (HAPS), the French Government donated No.15 (NX611), agreeing to deliver it to Bankstown, NSW, while HAPS set about fund-raising to bring the Lanc home. The history of this machine is well documented elsewhere in this issue, but briefly as G-ASXX she was ferried to the UK, arriving at Biggin Hill on May 13, 1965. Despite HAPS's many hopes for the Lanc, NX611 was to fly only 14 times in the UK, often finding a new base of operations.

With the demise of HAPS came another operator, Reflectaire and the last flight, into Blackpool, on June 26, 1970. From here the fortunes of the Lanc — and the rest of the collection — went downhill. This was reversed when she was acquired by Lord Lilford, NX611 was presented to the RAF in 1972, refurbished and put on gate guard duty at Scampton, Lincs. From there she was acquired by the Panton brothers and now forms the centre-piece of the Lincolnshire Aviation Heritage Centre at East Kirkby where the former Gallic Lancaster delights visitors, occasionally taxiing.

With all this preservation activity going on, it became apparent to a die-hard group of enthusiasts in France, that in all its generosity, France had overlooked itself in handing out Lancasters! Ailes Anciennes Ile de France realised that there was one former Aéronavale Lanc left, albeit in poor condition and on the other side of the world! This was No.21 (NX664) which had been badly damaged while landing on a strip at Mata Utu on the Wallis Islands on January 21, 1963. She had been stripped of useful spares to keep Nos.13 and 15 going and was long forgotten.

An epic fund-raising and recovery operation came to a climax in 1984 when No.21 was returned to Le Bourget (home of the Musée de l'Air) and where the Lanc had been overhauled by UTA in times gone by. An extensive restoration is still underway on No.21 with the volunteers of Ailes Anciennes looking forward to the day when the Lanc will join the long list of other types on display at the Musée.

Since the days of the Lancaster recovery from Polynesia, the French aviation heritage world is a lot sharper. It will endeavour to ensure that next time the baby is not thrown out with the bath water!